How to Mend a Broken Heart

How to Mend a Broken Heart

20 Active Ways to Healing

Dick Innes

Fleming H. Revell
A Division of Baker Book House Co
Grand Rapids, Michigan 49516

© 1994 by Dick Innes

Published by Revell Books
a division of Baker Book House Company
P.O. Box 6287, Grand Rapids, MI 49516-6287

Previously published in 1991 by Albatross Books (Australia) and Lion Publishing
(England).

Library of Congress Cataloging-in-Publication Data

Innes, Dick.
    How to mend a broken heart : 20 active ways to healing / Dick Innes.
— 1st Baker ed.
      p. cm.
    ISBN 0-8007-5501-4
    1. Loss (Psychology) 2. Loss (Psychology)—Religious aspects—Chris-
tianity. 3. Grief. I. Title
    BF575.D35I55 1994
    155.9' 37—dc20   94-1887

Printed in the United States of America

Contents

Preface

ojo: Para mi !

THIS BOOK IS FOR THOSE who have lost a loved one through death, divorce, or the breakdown of a romance.

People who have experienced such sorrows and losses are the ones who seem often to be able to understand life the most, understand people the most, and to care the most.

Loss is a part of life. Sooner or later it comes to us all. It need not impoverish us, but can enrich us. It need not hurt us, but can help us grow. And that is the purpose of this book—to help the reader make sense out of sorrow, to profit from pain, to grow through grief, and to turn sadness into gladness.

It is written out of my own experience and my search to make sense out of sorrow and loss.

It is written to assure those who are suffering the loss of a loved one that they, too, can work through their pain and come out as healthier and happier people whose lives have been greatly enriched. It is to ensure such people that they can live and love again.

It is a fact of life that some of the greatest success stories have been written by people who, against seemingly overwhelming and often insurmountable odds, have accepted their losses and turned them into opportunities for personal growth and stepping stones on their pathway to success. You can do the same.

I express my sincere thanks to the many friends who have supported me through my losses and thereby helped me make the writing of this book possible.

If you would like further help, please write to me, Dick Innes, at ACTS INTERNATIONAL, P.O. Box 157, Claremont, CA 91711

Introduction

"I'M IN LOVE WITH ANOTHER WOMAN."

The words were icy cold. Like a biting arctic wind, they stung bitterly and cut deeply into Ruth's heart.

Roger and Ruth's home seemed to be a very happy one. During the twenty-eight years of their marriage, Roger had been successful in his profession, and Ruth was the center of the many activities that revolved around their home and community.

One beautiful spring day, Roger invited Ruth to a special lunch with him before she got involved in her busy afternoon's activities. As usual, they had a good time together and, as Ruth put it, "Roger was as affectionate as ever."

When Ruth came home late that afternoon she had a spring in her step. Before preparing the evening meal, she went into her bedroom to change and relax. As she laid her things on the bed, she noticed an envelope on the pillow with her name on it.

"How sweet," she mused to herself. "It's from Roger."

"Dearest Ruth," the note started. "You have been a wonderful wife and mother. I could never have asked for anything more."

For some unknown reason, Ruth became a little suspicious. "Why is Roger talking like this? I wonder what he is up to?"

She soon found out. After some more compliments, Roger continued, "But I'm in love with another woman. I've left home. You will hear from my lawyer very soon."

Ruth was shocked with stunned disbelief. Time stood still. An icy hand seemed to reach in and tighten around her heart and freeze it. Panic and terror gripped her. It took several days to get over the initial shock before the ice around her heart began to melt.

Then the tears came like a flood. She sobbed as if her heart would break. During the weeks that followed, she wandered around in a fog. She pleaded with Roger to come home. Their grown children did the same. But their pleas fell on deaf ears. Ruth was left with divorce papers, shattered dreams, and a broken heart.

Sadly, Ruth's is not an isolated case. Her story is being repeated many times every day—to your friends and mine. A broken-hearted husband called me last week and urged me to try and persuade his bride of less than a year to return to him.

A friend's wife all but collapsed and ended up in a hospital when her husband of thirty years told her he no longer wanted to be married to her as there was another woman in his life.

Perhaps you, too, know all too well the pain of a broken relationship. This could be the anguish of divorce, breakdown in a romance, or the devastating loss of a loved one through death—the destruction of any relationship, in fact, that we have seen as a vital part of our life.

If so, how can you pick up the pieces of your shattered dreams and broken life, go on, and turn your sorrow into joy and your sadness into singing? How do you mend your broken heart? How do you get over the loss of a love?

1

Acknowledge the Loss

JANET HAD BEEN MARRIED eleven years when her husband, Ron, told her that he didn't want to be married to her anymore. Janet took it extremely hard and refused to believe that he meant what he said.

Two years after he left, she was still in denial even though Ron was now married to another woman. Obviously she didn't deny that Ron had left, but she kept hanging onto the hope that someday he would return.

Being the caretaker type, Janet allowed Ron to keep coming to her whenever he needed help, especially financial help. Even though she was fully supporting herself and taking care of their children, she kept supporting Ron. She did this because she was unwilling to acknowledge her loss. Every time she gave Ron money or help, she hoped to hear him say he was leaving the other woman and coming back to her. But she never heard it. She was torturing herself.

"Why don't you get out and join a singles group," I suggested to Janet, "so you can at least have some kind of social life and make new friends?"

"I just don't want to admit that I'm single," she said. "I just can't do it."

"But you've been single for two years!" I said.

"I know," Janet said, "but I don't want to face it!"

What Janet didn't want to face was the pain that is a normal part of loss. As long as she kept telling herself that Ron would come back and kept hanging onto that hope, she didn't have to face the pain of her loss. The tragedy was that Janet's denial of reality made her emotionally ill. She even had to be hospitalized because of it. As somebody else has said, "It's not the truth that hurts us, but letting go of the lies."

Erich Fromm, famed psychoanalyst once said, "The psychic task which a person can and must set for himself is not to feel secure, but to be able to tolerate insecurity."

What Fromm is saying is that to overcome our insecurity we need to admit that we feel insecure. Insecurity is part and parcel of the human condition. Most of us struggle with it at some time or other. Once we accept this fact and admit that we feel insecure, we can stop struggling to prove to ourselves and others that we don't feel insecure. Furthermore, only as we accept our insecurity can we do anything about overcoming its effect on us.

The same principle applies to our relationship problems—divorce, broken romance, death of a loved one—or, for that matter, any other loss. We need to accept the fact that loss is a normal part of life. It comes to us all sooner or later. And when it comes, the sooner we admit our loss, the sooner we can recover from it.

To overcome our problems, then, we need to take the following three steps.

❏ *First, face the truth.*

The greatest enemy we have in resolving any problem is a denial of it. As long as we refuse to admit what has happened, we can never resolve it. M. Scott Peck says, "Emotional illness is avoiding reality at any cost. Mental health is accepting reality at any cost." When Jesus Christ said, "You will know the truth, and the truth will set you free," he gave us a law of life that is as real as the law of gravity and just as powerful. To know the truth means to acknowledge and accept it. This is the only way to personal freedom.

> *The path to recovery can*
> *be a long, steep climb,*
> *but it beats staying in*
> *the valley of despair.*

Admitting and accepting one's loss is thus essential for the healing of a broken heart. If this is your situation, no matter how painful it is, to find healing you need to acknowledge and accept the reality and intensity of your loss. Even though you may feel you can't handle the pain, assure yourself that you are strong enough to bear it, that you will survive, and that you will become a better person as a result.

You may be in shock for weeks. You may try to convince yourself that your loss hasn't happened and that your loved one will come back. He or she may. Chances are, however, they won't. If death is the cause, they obviously won't be back. If it's because of divorce, it's not likely they will come back either. If they do, it will be an unexpected bonus. Just don't expect or plan for it, otherwise it may add to your already overloaded store of pain and disappointment.

❏ *Second, avoid "what ifs."*

As shocking as it may have been, whatever has happened has happened. Unfortunately, you can't go back and do anything differently. You cannot change any of the past. Perhaps you already did the best you knew how. In any case, acknowledge any mistakes you've made, but don't be too hard on yourself. And don't torture yourself with, "what ifs." They can't help and will only add to your pain.

It takes time to heal a broken heart, a process that can only begin at the point where you accept the reality of your loss. Fortunately, in recent weeks we got Janet to do this. She joined our Thursday night support group and through role play (psychodrama) she finally acknowledged her loss, dealt with many of her pent-up and repressed feelings, and began the process to freedom and healing.

The next day when Ron called her for more help, Janet did not allow him to take advantage of her. She was kind but very firm; she said she would no longer take care of him and that she didn't want him to phone her anymore. She finally acknowledged the fact that this man had chosen to leave her and was married to another woman.

❏ *Third, take courage.*

Yes, the pain of Janet's loss was intense. It seemed as though it would overwhelm her. But as long as she denied it, she was stuck in her pain and was going nowhere with her life. But the moment she acknowledged her loss and stopped running from facing the pain, she was freed to begin the process of recovery. Now, for the first time since her divorce two years ago, Janet feels good about herself and is a new woman.

The change has been so dramatic that one of her staff at work said to her, "Janet, I don't know what has happened to you and I don't know what you do in this group you talk about, but whatever it is you've got, I want it. Can I come to your group with you?"

I've sat in other support groups where I have seen people stuck in their pain and crying, "Where is there hope?" They couldn't seem to find a way out of their dilemma. But there *is* hope for the hurting and the broken-hearted. It begins with acknowledging the truth of their loss.

The path to recovery can be a long, steep climb, but it beats staying in the valley of despair. And the view at the top is worth all the sweat and pain of the climb.

Acceptance of your loss is the very next step. Take it as soon as you can.

2

Accept Your Pain as Normal

"I CAN'T GET THIS WOMAN off my mind," Bruce said. "What can I do about it? We dated for three years and were planning on getting married. I had a business failure and she dropped me cold. That was months ago and I still can't get her out of my mind."

"That's understandable," I said. "When you go with someone for that amount of time and love them enough to want to marry them, the pull towards that person can seem irresistible, especially when a strong emotional bonding has taken place. When that person is suddenly taken out of your life, you quickly discover you just can't walk away from the relationship and check your feelings at the door."

If you are married and very much in love and your spouse dies or leaves you, the agony can be even more intense. One woman I know has been married for almost thirty years. Her husband had been running around on her. Each time she excused and forgave him. They finally separated, but she felt that she couldn't live without him. When he left, she understandably experienced intense pain. Instead of facing the pain and working through it, she gave in and had her husband come back without insisting that he get help to resolve his problem.

The only way out of pain is to go through it.

I'm not saying that she should or shouldn't have taken him back. What I am saying is this: Unless he faces and resolves his problem, he is bound to repeat his past behavior—especially if his wife lets him get away with it without serious consequences. Like everybody else, he will either resolve his past or repeat it.

It is very easy to do foolish things when we are hurting just to avoid facing and dealing with the pain. Some of us will do anything to avoid feeling our pain and then pay dearly for it later on.

For whatever reason you lose a loved one, the pain is very real. You go to bed at night with an overwhelming longing for the person you loved and lost. You get up in the morning feeling the same way. You miss them terribly. Days are long and lonely. Sleepless nights are filled with despair. Time drags. Weekends seem to last forever and are the worst times. A big part of your life is missing.

You cannot go through such traumas without experiencing deep pain. It may not feel like it at the time, but the pain can be resolved. To do this there are several steps you can take.

❏ *First, realize that it is normal to feel very hurt and to experience a devastating sense of loss.*

The pain you experience at a time of loss may seem overwhelming. It may seem more than you can bear. And, if you are the type of person who is addicted to relationships (there are many who are), you will experience actual withdrawal symptoms, the pain of which can be agonizing.

Either way, the pain is going to take time to heal. In a divorce or the death of a spouse, it can take months to work through the worst of the pain and a year or more to feel like your old self again. If, however, many months have passed and you don't seem to be coming to terms with your loss, it is important to get outside help such as that of a trained minister or counselor.

❏ *Second, know when enough is enough.*

If you have done everything humanly possible to resolve your relationship or regain your lost love and nothing has worked and love is lost, make the decision to accept your loss so you can face and resolve it and get on with your life.

I recently heard about one woman who, after fourteen years of marriage, got a divorce. "Why did you get divorced?" a friend asked. She replied, "My husband has been physically beating me."

"But he's been doing that for the last fourteen years. Why did you decide to leave him now?"

"Because I came to the realization that I don't deserve that kind of treatment any longer. Enough is enough."

When it's time to face a bad scene, face it and accept the pain of your loss. You don't deserve the kind of treatment we've just talked about, either. I'm not recommending divorce. That should only be a last resort after all else has failed. What I am recommending is this: If your relationship has broken down, don't deny the reality of your circumstances as a way of avoiding the pain. Be a positive realist; acknowledge the bad situation and face the hurt, knowing that the only way out of pain is to go through it.

❏ *Third, choose your beliefs carefully.*

Our beliefs have a direct and profound effect on how we feel and act. For example, if you believe that you can't live without the person you have lost, that belief will control your actions, thoughts, and feelings. It will keep you depressed and bogged down in self-pity and will block your recovery.

We may not always live what we *profess,* but we always live consistently with what we *believe.* Not to live the life we believe means that we end up unhappily believing the life we live. This is because the mind cannot remain in harmony or at peace with itself when we live inconsistently with our belief system. If we try to do so, we experience what the experts call "cognitive dissonance," which simply means mental disharmony. To maintain mental harmony, we change our beliefs to match the life we are living. This is to keep us living consistently with our beliefs. Even the most hardened criminal believes what he is doing is justified.

Our beliefs are like a built-in automatic pilot. They direct our total life. If we believe we are unlovable, we will act in an unlovable manner. If we believe we are a failure, we will set ourselves up to fail. If we believe we are basically bad, we will act bad. Conversely, if we believe we are lovable, we will act in a loving manner. Life is a series of belief choices, and we are in a sense the sum total of all those choices. We believe what we choose to believe, what we want to believe.

If we choose to believe, therefore, that we can't get over our loss, we handicap our recovery. If we believe we can overcome it, we assist it. The choice is ours. It's in our hands. So choose your beliefs carefully.

❏ *Fourth, if you've called it quits, make sure you quit.*

Don't give in to the temptation to keep running back—either in reality or in your fantasies—to the person who hurt you. Don't keep hanging onto false hope. This is what Ruth, whom we talked about in the introduction, was still doing three years after her husband left her. Instead of accepting her pain and working through it, she kept living in the past as a way of avoiding and not dealing with her loss.

If you keep on going back to the person who hurt you and there is no change in their behavior and feelings toward you, you are keeping yourself locked in your pain and will never be able to resolve it.

❏ *Fifth, feel your pain.*

Don't deny, withdraw, or run from your pain. To heal it you have to feel it. There is no other way, so accept the fact that it hurts to lose a loved one and that you are going to experience painful feelings. As already pointed out, the way out of the pain is through it. There is no way around it, so accept the emotions you are feeling so you can work through them. Some people withdraw, hoping the pain will go away. It doesn't. Others deny their pain and repress it from conscious memory. This causes greater pain and problems at a later time. Still others turn to such forms of addictive behavior as drugs, alcohol, overwork, sex, spending, gambling, and religion to anesthetize their pain. These don't take it away either. They save it up to bring it back another day with interest.

By denying our pain now we can have short-term gain for long-term pain; by facing our pain now we can have short-term pain for long-term gain.

❑ *Finally, expect the best and go for it.*

Some people who have been hooked on alcohol may abstain from drinking for a number of years, but when something goes wrong in their life they easily slip back into their old drinking habits. Why do they do this when they know the problems their drinking caused in the past? Psychiatrists tell us the difference lies in moving from being an abstainer to experiencing the joy of sobriety. Until the alcoholic makes this transition, he is vulnerable and leaves himself open to falling again.

It's the same with relationships. The goal needs to be not just to "abstain" or be separated from the lost love, but to resolve the loss and pain so you can be free to experience the joy of living fully beyond that loss, and to grow richer because of it. Others have done this. You can, too.

3

Realize That This, Too, Will Pass

NEIL AND JOY HAD WORKED HARD for many years to establish their home, build up their business, and raise their family of three children. During their marriage of twenty-seven years, they had faced and overcome their share of personal conflicts, had survived two major business setbacks, and had recently experienced the loss of their last child leaving home.

While they felt the pain of the last child leaving the nest, they were happy for their children and were very much looking forward to being able to spend more time together. They also hoped to take an overseas trip, which had been their desire for many years.

The week after their daughter left home, Neil phoned Joy to say he was on his way home from work and would be home shortly. But Neil never arrived. His car was hit head-on by a drunk driver and Neil was killed instantly.

Joy was understandably devastated. That was fifteen months ago. Overcoming her loss has not been easy, but little by little the wound of her heart has been healing. At first she was angry at God, blaming him for what had happened. She was also very angry at the drunk driver who came out of the accident with little more than a few cuts and bruises. And she was angry at the law, because the man who killed her husband received only a very light sentence. At times she thought she would never recover. Every memory of Neil for the next few months brought another flood of tears.

As rainbows are painted by rain, so faith, hope, and love are all painted by pain.

Fortunately, Joy realized that she needed help and joined a support group to help her work through the pain of her loss. She now realizes that it wasn't God who was responsible for the loss of her husband, and she has resolved her anger. The last time I talked to her, her face was beaming. She is well on the road to recovery and in the process of rebuilding her life.

Recently, I asked another friend who has been divorced for five years if she felt that she had fully recovered. She told me that the first year or two were very difficult, but she feels good about herself again. She has gone back to college to upgrade her training and improve her qualifications. She is very positive about the future and is confident that she has fully recovered from her divorce. She also feels she is a much better person as a result of her painful experience.

Most of the trials of life pass. If we look back, we realize that we have all come through difficulties in the past—from a broken heart as a teenager, an accident that may have laid us up for several weeks or months, a sickness, depression, a financial setback, the loss of a job, and so on.

At the time we may have feared our trials would never end and that we would never be any good ever again. But it wasn't so. We discovered that *time* was the great healer and that 90 percent of the things we feared never happened—and the worry we invested in the rest didn't help anyhow. They passed, too, and we survived.

Human suffering is part of the human condition. We just happen to live in a broken world where, as the Bible says, the sun rises on good people as well as on evil ones, and rain falls on just people as well as unjust ones. Or, as the songwriter expressed it, "Into each life some rain must fall."

The good thing about rain is that it brings new life. Without it there is no growth, only desert. It is the rain as well as the sunshine that produces lush growth. It's the same with life: Pain as well as joy—rain as well as sunshine—is needed to produce growth and maturity. Furthermore, without rain there are no rainbows either. As rainbows are painted by rain, so faith, hope, and love are all painted by pain.

Another good thing about rain is that it always passes, and in most places there is always a lot more sunshine than rain.

The whole of life is a cycle. Sunshine always follows rain. Calm follows storms. Morning follows night. Winter follows fall. Fall follows summer. Summer follows spring. And spring always follows winter—without exception.

Just as certain is the fact that your night of sorrow will pass and you will find joy in the morning. The winter of your discontent that you are going through now will, in its own time, also pass.

Be assured, you will smile and sing again. Not only will you sing again but, if you use your pain as an opportunity to grow, you can become a much better person as a result. You will become more sensitive, more aware, more understanding, more sympathetic, stronger, wiser—and discover a much greater appreciation of life and other people.

The ancient psalmist was correct when he said, "Weeping may remain for a night, but joy comes in the morning."

It will for you, too.

4

Don't Waste
Your Pain

BEFORE JOHN'S FIRST SON was born over twenty-one years
ago, Barbara, his wife, broke down emotionally and went
into a deep depression which plagued her and her family for
the next twenty years.

Like so many women (and men) in today's society,
Barbara was a victim of sexual abuse at the hand of a trusted
family friend. She was only two-and-a-half years old when
the abuse began. The victimizer also terrorized her by threatening to kill her with a very sharp knife if ever she revealed
their secret. The experience was so traumatic for such a
young child that she totally repressed the trauma from her
conscious mind.

The great tragedy with such experiences is that they are
never buried dead, but very much alive. The stuff that is
shoved underground never goes away; it just builds up and
comes back with accrued interest. This is why it is so impor-

tant to resolve painful emotions as close as possible to the time of the event that caused them in the first place.

For the next eighteen years, John and Barbara went to counselor after counselor seeking relief from the tormenting depression. It took a complete breakdown, several hospitalizations, a massive stroke at thirty-seven—which complicated matters and added to the depression—and years of therapy before the pieces of the buried past came back to conscious memory. Even then there was no relief from the debilitating depression except for short periods.

The pain passes, but the beauty remains.

John and Barbara were both well-educated and had a deep commitment to the Christian faith. Outwardly, they looked like the perfect couple. Only close friends knew the struggles they were facing. For the next ten years, every therapist and doctor they went to gave up, saying there was nothing more they could do for them.

Little by little, Barbara's condition worsened. After nearly eight more years of therapy, new counselors also gave up, saying there was nothing more they could do. For almost twenty years, John and Barbara tried everything humanly possible— spiritual as well as secular—to find a cure. Nothing worked. They didn't make it—together. Divorce was the only thing that finally brought relief.

The question that comes to mind in such situations is this: Were the twenty years of John and Barbara's struggle wasted?

According to John, those years seemed like a never-ending nightmare. "Over and over," he said, "my heart cried, 'Where are you, God, when it hurts so bad?' Year after year our trials were like ocean waves. They kept coming and coming with relentless regularity and at times almost overwhelmed me. Time and again I asked, 'Is there any sense in all that is happening to us? Will any good ever come out of this?'

"But my trial did pass," John said. "Through it all I've learned some invaluable lessons. I've learned that pain can be a great teacher, a powerful motivator, and a profound enricher of life." Let us look at each of these in turn.

❑ *First, pain can be a great teacher.*

"As I look back," John now acknowledges, "I didn't learn about life in school, in books, or at church, but in the twenty-year wilderness of disappointment and the desert of loss and heartbreak."

John is convinced that if there is any quality in the work he is doing today it has come out of this twenty-year trial. "That is where I learned about life, about people, and about the suffering and sorrows that people face every day," he says. "Wisdom, insight, and an understanding of life and people often have to be learned at the College of Hard Knocks.

"I'd hate to go through the last twenty years again, but I am very grateful for the lessons about life that I have learned during this time. I am equally grateful for the work that I have been given to do—a work that helps many more face and overcome their personal struggles, conflicts, losses, and hurts. I constantly thank God for this opportunity for the lessons learned through pain to help qualify me for this work. Pain such as I have been through should never be wasted, but worked through and then invested in the growth and healing of other people."

I am convinced it is one thing to hurt, but it's something else to hurt and waste the pain of any bad experience. The truth is, pain can make us or break us. It can be a great teacher of life or it can make us disillusioned with life. In other words, pain can make us bitter or it can make us better. The choice is ours. As John says, we can waste our pain or we can invest it. In all crises it isn't so much what happens to us that is important, but how we react to what happens.

The Chinese have two characters for the word "crisis." One is danger, the other opportunity. What they are saying is that in every crisis and loss there is the danger of becoming bitter or the opportunity of becoming better. We decide which road we will take: the bitter road or the better road.

Not to take the better road and use our pain as an opportunity to enrich our lives, to grow, and to enrich the lives of others makes of pain a tragic waste.

❏ *Second, pain can be a great motivator.*

Pain is nature's way of letting us know that something is wrong and needs attention. It is a self-protective device. When a bone breaks, it hurts. If it didn't hurt, chances are we wouldn't take proper care of it and it wouldn't heal properly.

Without any pain, life would be extremely hazardous. For instance, the first symptom of high cholesterol, which of itself has no pain, can be sudden death by a heart attack. One of the dangers of leprosy is the loss of feeling and pain. A person with this disease hurts his foot, but because he feels no pain, he has nothing to remind him to protect his wounded limb. He hurts it again. And again. Still there's no pain. Eventually he loses his foot.

Thank God for pain. It's an impelling force to aid the healing process and motivate us to take proper care of ourselves when we are hurting. It is also one of the most effective motivators to cause us to look at ourselves and deal with our personal problems, resolve our past, and to grow and mature. One of the worst things we can do with our pain is to run away from it. We need to accept it and invest it—not only in helping other hurting people, but in our own growth and maturity.

This is why the Bible says, "Dear brothers [and sisters], is your life full of difficulties and temptations? Then be happy, for when the way is rough, your patience has a chance to grow. So let it grow, and don't try to squirm out of your problems. For when your patience is finally in full bloom, then you will be ready for anything, strong in character, full and complete."

❏ *Third, pain can be a great enricher of life.*

There's something else invaluable about pain, too. It can make you more sensitive, more compassionate, more understanding, and more creative.

Beethoven, for instance, composed one of his greatest oratorios after he became deaf. John Milton wrote one of his greatest poems after he became blind. Walter Scott wrote "The Lay of the Last Minstrel" after he was kicked by a horse and was confined to his house for many days.

Those who have given the world the most are often those who have suffered the most. This is because those who have suffered the most tend to understand life and people the most.

One of my favorite stories is told about Renoir, the famous French painter. Apparently, when he was older, he suffered greatly from arthritis, but he kept painting anyhow. On one occasion his friend, Matisse, said to him, "Renoir, my friend, why do you keep painting when you are in so much pain?"

Renoir simply replied, "The pain passes, but the beauty remains."

When it comes to your pain, if you invest it wisely by using it to help yourself grow and reach out to nurture other hurting people, your pain, too, will pass, but the beauty of what you have done will remain forever.

Remember, it's one thing to hurt. It's another thing to allow your pain to hurt you. Accept your hurt as an opportunity to heal, to grow, and to become a more understanding, sensitive, compassionate, and creative person. It has been costly. Don't waste it. Invest it wisely in your own growth and in the enrichment of other people's lives as well.

5

Give Yourself
Time to Heal

"I BELIEVE IN MIRACLES, but not magic," a friend of mine likes to say. I agree. Magic is wanting an instant fix. Miracles take a little longer—usually a lot longer.

Unfortunately, there are no such things as instant fixes. Like get-rich-quick schemes, they rarely if ever work. Healing takes time. If we try to push the process too fast, we only hurt ourselves.

❏ *First, go with God's timing.*

What we need to remember is that God is never in a hurry. It is we who are in a hurry and get impatient for quick results.

When I first started the work I am now in over twenty years ago, I thought I could do all I wanted to do in ten years. It didn't take long, however, to realize that it was going to take me a lifetime to do a lifetime's work! Many people have ruined their chances for true success because they weren't prepared to hang in for the long haul. They wanted a quick fix.

A problem in this day of fast cars, fast living, fast food, and the desire for immediate gratification is a great desire on the part of many for instant success, instant wealth, instant healing, instant maturity, and instant recovery from pain. There is no such thing. In spite of today's advanced technology and scientific knowledge, there are *still* no quick fixes. Healing is a process. Trust your life to God and go with his timing and you will receive his blessings.

---

*Broken bones may heal
in six weeks.
Broken hearts don't.*

❑ *Second, take time to resolve your past.*

In my work and other links with people I see some people rushing into marriage. I see some rushing out of it. I then see some rushing back into another marriage without ever taking the time to recover from the first one, and without making the effort to resolve the causes within themselves that contributed to their first marriage breakup . . . and their second . . . and sometimes their third. It is a fact of life that we either take time to resolve our past or we are destined to repeat it!

One man I know, whom I will call Michael, is on his fourth marriage. In his latest, he and his new wife were hardly unpacked when they were in serious conflict. His bride of only a few weeks left him, threatening never to return.

Michael came for counseling, and I suggested that he examine his previous relationships to gain insights into why his marriages kept failing. One thing was evident: Each wife abandoned him. At first he wanted to place the blame for this on the women he married.

"Well," I asked, "even if it were completely their fault, why did you choose this type of woman? Why does every woman you are attracted to run away? Is this a coincidence? Did anyone in your early life abandon you either physically or emotionally?"

"Yes," Michael said, "both my mother and father did. When they were unhappy with me, they would tie me up to a post in the basement of our home and leave me. I was terrified."

Unconsciously, Michael was still looking for a woman to fill his empty childhood love tank and was choosing women just like his mother. In other words, he was looking for a substitute mother to meet the need his own mother never met. No wife can ever do that—especially the type of women Michael kept choosing.

No sooner is Michael out of one relationship than he runs to another, without ever taking the time to face and resolve his abandonment issue which has its roots in his early childhood.

Instead of facing his pain, he runs to another "substitute mother" in order to anesthetize his pain, ever hoping that the present woman will make him happy. She *never* will. Happiness has its roots within oneself, never without. Only happy people make happy marriages.

Much of what we call love is overdependent need. This is Michael's problem. Instead of needing a woman because he loves her, he "loves" her because he needs her . . . as a pacifier to silence his pain.

As long as Michael is in a relationship with a woman, he doesn't have to face his feelings of abandonment. As soon as this woman walks out on him, however, he experiences not only the pain of her abandonment but the even more intense pain of his mother's abandonment. To avoid facing this double load of pain, he compulsively latches onto another woman (with her own set of problems). And the vicious cycle continues.

Michael is a love addict. Women are his drug of choice. This is because any compulsive behavior that is used to avoid facing pain is an addiction. Unless Michael takes a good, hard look at himself and takes the time to resolve his abandonment issue, he will continue to repeat the same pattern and will keep being drawn to women who will abandon him—just like his mother did.

Fortunately, Michael is now in counseling as his load of pain became more than he could bear. Hopefully, this time he will take the time and make the effort to resolve his past.

Even if your pain may not be as intense as Michael's, it is critical that you take time to resolve your past before getting involved in any other "permanent" relationship.

❏ *Third, allow nature to take its course.*

When it comes to loss, you don't live with a person for many years and lose them without suffering deep wounds. And, like any wound, the deeper it is, the greater the time it takes to heal.

Broken bones may heal in six weeks. Broken hearts don't. Sometimes the healing can seem discouragingly slow, but if your loss was a year or more ago, look back and consider how far you've come and how much you've grown already. It's usually much better than it seems. Think, too, how much more you will grow in the next six months . . . twelve months.

It can take a year or even more to heal from the loss of a loved one or recover from divorce. A big part of your life has been cut out. It's much more than a broken bone. It's major surgery. It hurts. It takes time to heal—a lot of time. So be kind to and patient with yourself. Don't demand more of yourself than you would of someone else.

It's a rough sea you're passing through. There are lots of ups and downs. One day you feel fine and think you're getting into calmer waters. The next day, or even by nightfall, the emotional seas are pitching wildly once again. Realize that your ups and downs are normal and be assured that in time you will reach the shelter of calmer waters.

Nature has its own time schedule. You can't push it. A scratch heals in a few days. A broken bone takes six weeks. You can't speed either one up, but you can take good care of the wound, doing what you can to facilitate its healing and letting nature take its course by giving it the time it requires to heal.

The same principle applies to healing wounds of the heart. You can't speed up the process, but you can stop it from taking longer than necessary—by taking good care of yourself, doing what you can to facilitate your healing, and giving yourself permission to take time to heal.

Nature isn't in a hurry. God isn't either. His word to you today is, "Be still, and know that I am God."

You need to be still in your heart and know that you will survive . . . that in time you will heal . . . that you will become a better, stronger person . . . and that if you trust your life to God, he will bring you safely through the storm.

It is true: All things do work together for good to those who love and trust God—even if it is eventually.

6
Do Your Grieving Now

IMAGINE GOING TO SEE a hilariously funny movie where it isn't acceptable or permissible to laugh. Or being at the championship match of a football game when there is only thirty seconds left to play. The score is even. Your team's halfback has the ball and is running frantically toward the end zone with only three yards to go. Seven of the opposing team are all on top of him—and it isn't permissible for the spectators to yell and scream!

If we were never allowed to laugh at things that are funny or yell when we are excited it probably would kill us. Literally.

For some reason, in our culture it's okay for women to express their emotions and it's okay for both men and women to laugh at things that are funny and to yell and scream at sports events, but it's not okay for men to cry.

By the time I was five years of age, I was taught that big men don't cry. The fallacy with this teaching is that a little boy of five is not a big man. The other fallacy is that big men do cry. It's frightened men who don't cry—men who were taught that to cry was a sign of weakness.

When a little boy is hurt he is told to stop crying or he will be given something to cry about. Or when he falls and hurts himself he is told to be a big man and not cry. Over and over he gets the message that boys don't cry and, by the time he is a teenager, he doesn't dare show his tears when he is hurt. Tragically, as an adult he has lost the ability to cry even at times of severe loss. Men then excuse their inability to cry on the grounds that they are being strong. It may be stoic, but that isn't being strong. It's being crazy.

I can still remember the day my little sister died. I was only five at the time and she was nineteen months old. We loved each other dearly. I recall how we would play hide-and-seek. She would hide behind the sofa and, when I would find her, she would squeal with delight. Suddenly she took ill, was rushed to hospital, and never came back. The loss for me was devastating but, because "big men don't cry," on the day of her funeral when somebody asked me how I felt, I laughed it off and said I felt fine. I buried my grief very well—but I was lying.

Thirty-some years later, along with many other repressed emotions, this incident caught up with me. I had bursitis in both shoulders and couldn't lift my arms without pain. I had miserable hay-fever attacks every year and other physical ills. I also felt like I was drying up on the inside and was having trouble with close relationships.

Then I went for counseling. I had no idea I had so much repressed anger and hurt. Out it came. And when I got in touch with the grief over the loss of my little sister, I sobbed for days. What relief to get these bottled-up feelings out into the open where they should have been when I was only five.

An unexpected bonus was that, when I emptied out these feelings, I was healed physically!

---

*Don't bottle up your
feelings and thereby
erect a brick wall
around your heart.*

The fact is that God gave us laughter to express joy and fun, a voice to yell with at times of intense excitement, and tears to express our grief and sorrow. One of the most damaging things we can do with these emotions is to bottle them up and bury them. If we bury them, we never bury them dead, but very much alive. Sooner or later they will come back to haunt us . . . perhaps disguised as floating anxiety, depression, ulcers, arthritis, heart problems, cancer—or a score of other physical and psychological ills, in destructive behavior, or in more broken relationships.

Whatever you do, don't deny or run away from your emotions by escaping into harmful activities or damaging habits. Don't escape into too many good activities or unnecessary busyness either. Do your grieving now. The following suggestions might help.

❏ *First, give yourself permission to feel.*

The critical thing to do is to recognize what emotions you are experiencing, admit what they are, accept them and then express them as soon as possible. This cleans out the emotional wound and makes healing possible. Bottled up, they are like dirt in a wound that causes infection and stops the healing process.

In times of loss, besides feeling intense sorrow, it's normal to feel afraid, angry and even guilty. Give yourself permission to feel *all* your emotions, express them creatively and work through the various stages of grief—from shock and denial, through intense hurt, loneliness, depression—experiencing physical symptoms from the distress, fear and panic, guilt, anger and resentment until you finally come to understanding, acceptance and peace and back to living normally once again.

❏ *Second, you can express your emotions by talking them out, crying them out, and/or writing them out once you are in touch with them.*

If you write your feelings out (and you don't have to send a copy to anyone), write to the person who hurt you, left you, fired you, or died. Tell them exactly how you feel.

Or, when driving in your car, wind the windows up, turn the radio on, and imagine the person you are grieving over is sitting there beside you. Tell them how much you are hurting. Share your anger with them for leaving you: your hurt, your fear, your guilt, and any other emotions you may be experiencing. Should you feel a need to send a letter to the person who hurt you, never ever send the first draft! Or find a trusted friend with whom you can bare your soul, join a group where you can express your feelings without any fear of being judged and, if necessary, seek the help of a trained counselor.

Just don't bottle up your feelings and thereby erect a brick wall around your heart. The wound in your heart needs cleaning out. If you cover it over and pretend that it doesn't exist or think that it will take care of itself, your buried emotions can readily poison your health and infect all your relationships.

When you suffer a deep loss, it's normal to feel bad. If you don't feel any pain at the time of your loss or within a few days, you may have repressed your emotions. If you have done this, I strongly suggest you see a trained counselor right away. If you don't recognize your pain and deal with it now, as sure as night follows day it will come back to torment you at a later date.

By failing to face the pain now, you will force your emotions below the level of consciousness, only to have them erupt at a later stage, even years later, in destructive ways. If you are going to avoid certain disaster in the future, it is imperative that you face and resolve your painful feelings now.

❏ *Third, to heal your emotions you need to feel them.*

Talking or writing about emotions is not enough. To heal them you need to feel them, then *express* them. Supercharged, repressed, negative emotions are poison to your physical, emotional, and spiritual health. They need to be acknowledged, identified for exactly what they are, owned, *felt* in all their intensity, and expressed in appropriate ways.

If you're hurting, don't just talk about it: cry! If you're angry, don't just talk about that either: feel and verbalize, or write out the anger . . . and so on. When you do this, you can be assured that these emotions, as overpowering as they may feel today, will eventually dissipate and pass.

The more you feel and deal with them now, the less you will suffer later. So don't postpone your grieving. Make sure you do it now.

7

Let Go
of the Past

I ONCE READ ABOUT TWO MONKS who were returning home from a journey to a distant abbey. It was a dismal, rainy day. On rounding a bend on the way, they came to a swollen stream which was threatening to overflow its banks. Standing by the stream was a beautiful woman too nervous to chance the flooded crossing for fear she might get swept away.

"Allow me to carry you across the stream," said one of the monks, as he picked her up and carried her safely to the other side.

Later that night the other monk suddenly blurted out, "I think you made a grave mistake today picking up that woman. You know we are not to have any dealings with the opposite sex."

"How strange," remarked the monk. "I carried her only across the stream. You are carrying her still."

Unfortunately, many grieving people are still carrying the person they lost. I was talking to one woman this past week who was divorced over two years ago. Every week she attended a function that she felt sure her ex-husband would appreciate when he came back to her, even though he had already remarried.

> *Life can only be understood by looking backward, but it must be lived by looking forward.*

Holding on to the past makes recovery impossible. Admittedly, it can be very difficult to let go of those things that were dear to us and especially difficult to let go of persons who were precious to us. I know one man whose wife walked out on him three years ago. Every time I talk to him, he keeps going back to the day his wife left him. That's where he is stuck. He is still very bitter about what happened and has never dealt with his hurt or anger or faced what he contributed to his marriage breakup. What he fails to see is that, as long as he just talks about his grief and never lets go of it, he will never resolve it.

Letting go of the past is essential for recovering the loss of a love. To do so there are several steps one needs to take.

❏ *First, want to let go of the past.*

People often get confused between the words "can't" and "don't want." A friend whose grandmother just passed away told me she just couldn't get out and mix with our friends. I asked why and she said that it was because she was afraid she couldn't be strong in front of people.

"Do you mean by being strong that you don't want to let anybody see you cry?" I asked.

"Yes," she said.

"You know that's not true, don't you?" I said. "Is it that you couldn't get out or that you didn't want to get out?"

She admitted that she didn't want to get out. How self-defeating it is when people confuse not crying with being strong. And how self-defeating it is when we keep telling ourselves that we *can't* get out or *can't* do anything else. When we tell ourselves "we can't," that's what we believe and it paralyzes us.

More often than not, "I can't" is a handy excuse to hang on to if we want to cling to the past. To overcome our heartache it is essential that we genuinely *want* to and make the decision that we are going to.

❏ *Second, stop blaming yourself.*

"It's all my fault. It's all my fault that my husband left me," Joyce kept repeating. "If only I'd been a better wife and taken better care of my husband, he would never have left me."

Rarely, if ever, is a marriage breakup the fault of one person. Besides, I happen to know Joyce's ex-husband and know that their breakup wasn't all Joyce's fault. If anything, I'd say it was more the other way around. Socially Joyce was somewhat shy and her husband didn't like this. He constantly pushed her to be more outgoing and to be something that she wasn't. He did it for his sake, not hers. Joyce's biggest "fault," if you could call it that, was to believe her husband's demands were justified.

A teenager whom I shall call Mary was still grieving over the fact that she had broken off a relationship with a young man. He had done something stupid after they had broken up and ended up in jail. She was blaming herself for his being sent to jail. I assured her that she had nothing to do with his behavior. He chose to do what he did and was totally responsible for it.

Mary's weakness is that, like so many of us, she is a co-dependent. Co-dependents feel they are responsible for what happens to the people in their lives and tend to feel they are to blame for all that goes bad for them. Co-dependents need to be needed in order to feel loved and want to "fix" the needy people they are attracted to. When they fail to fix them (which they can't), they feel they are to blame. To let go of your loss, admit what you did contribute but don't take the blame for everything that went wrong.

❑ *Third, resolve your feelings now.*

We discussed the importance of releasing our painful emotions in the last chapter. The importance of taking this step cannot be overemphasized, because it is our supercharged repressed negative emotions that, perhaps more than anything else, keep us from letting go of the past. In fact, as long as we keep those painful emotions locked inside of us, we are bound by the past.

❑ *Fourth, plan what you are going to do with the rest of your life and set new directions, purposes, and goals.*

According to many studies, less than 3 percent of all people have a specific purpose and major goal for their life. Without these, we are like a boat without a rudder. The storms of life hit us and we bounce around like a cork, not knowing where we are going to end up.

For people who have a specific purpose for their life and a major goal, the storms of life may batter them around a bit and they may feel like they've taken a beating, but they always bounce back. They know where they are going and how they are going to get there, and they use every circumstance that comes their way—good or bad—as a stepping stone and as a means to better equip them to get to where they are going with their life.

If you don't have a specific purpose and major goal for your life, I suggest that you resolve to formulate these within the next twenty-one days. Start them today. Do it now. Write them down. Once you have emptied out your painful feelings, there is nothing that will help you to let go of the past and get you on the road to recovery more quickly than having something worthwhile to live for into which you can put your best and most creative efforts.

❏ *Fifth, begin working toward the fulfillment of your purpose and the achievement of your goals immediately.*

Think of Candy Lightner, the founder of the organization, MADD (Mothers Against Drunk Drivers). Candy's teenage daughter was killed by a drunken driver who received little more than a rap on his knuckles for the crime he committed. Candy didn't allow her grief to leave her bitter—angry, yes, and rightfully so, but not bitter.

Candy made up her mind that she was going to do everything she could to get drunk drivers off the road. That gave her a purpose to live for and a goal to work toward. She put together an organization to fight drunk drivers. As a result, many laws were tightened and the penalty for drunk driving stiffened. Even though the problem of drunk driving hasn't been solved, many lives have been saved because of one woman's purpose and determination. Candy Lightner chose not to waste her pain, but to use it to achieve a much higher purpose with her life.

As already stated, it takes time to resolve feelings of grief and to cross the stream of your flooded emotions and adjust to your new circumstances. To recover, you have three basic choices.

First, even though you can't go back and relive your life, in your mind you can easily live in the past, never let go of it, and never truly heal. Second, you can deal with your painful feelings and resolve them, but stand still and not go anywhere with your life. Or third, through a conscious choice and determined effort you can resolve your past, let go of it, and then move forward and achieve with your life things you never dreamed possible.

As has been wisely said, "Life can only be understood by looking backward, but it must be lived by looking forward."

That's great advice. Look back only to understand and resolve your past and put it behind you. But look forward to a bright, happy, fulfilling tomorrow. Say to yourself, "I have been hurt, but through it I am learning more about life, I am becoming a more aware and better person. My life is being enriched. I am growing. Now it is time to move on."

You don't have to wait until all your grieving is done. You can start letting go of your past right away. You can do this by not dwelling on it any more than is necessary to resolve it, but by thinking about your new future and being thankful for that. And, like the monk who carried the stranded woman across the flooded stream, once you have crossed your stream, lay your burden down, let go of it, and leave it behind you.

Of one thing you can be certain: God does have a purpose for your life. It's in your future, not your past. He wants you to find it. Only then will you find true and lasting fulfillment.

8

Forgive
to Be Free

LEONARDO DA VINCI was not only an extremely gifted artist, but also a very capable draftsman, engineer, and thinker. Just before he commenced working on one of his masterpieces, "The Last Supper," he apparently had a very bitter quarrel with a fellow painter.

So enraged and resentful was Leonardo that he determined to paint the face of the hated artist into the face of Judas, the one who betrayed Christ. This was one of the first faces he completed.

But when he came to paint the face of Christ, he lost all inspiration and couldn't make any progress, no matter how hard he tried. He finally realized that it was his unresolved resentment toward his fellow artist that was causing his mental block. He then proceeded to repaint the face of Judas, painting out the face of his enemy. In so doing he was freed and went on to paint the face of Jesus and complete the painting, the success of which has been recognized through the centuries.

To fail to forgive is to be bound by the past. And, as already noted, in most broken relationships, even those broken through death, there is not only hurt but often unresolved anger and resentment.

If we fail to resolve our past, we are destined to repeat it.

To be free to grow, to move ahead and to heal your broken heart, it is essential to forgive the person who hurt, deserted or left you. One of the greatest obstacles, however, to forgiveness is anger.

To forgive doesn't mean that you deny your anger and sweep it under the rug. Not at all. You deal with and resolve the anger first, otherwise you won't be able to truly forgive. You cannot ice over anger with forgiveness. If you try, the anger will keep rearing its ugly head. It may also turn into resentment and bitterness. Deal with the anger first—admit it, confess it, express it creatively, get it out of your system— then the way is open to forgive.

The question is often asked, How can I deal with my anger and get it out of my system so I can freely forgive?

❏ *First, identify your anger.*

One of the most difficult things to do when we have lost a loved one, especially through death, is to recognize anger. "How could I possibly be angry at someone who died?" I reason to myself. "It wasn't their fault. And how can I be angry at somebody I love?"

The answer is very easy. Unfortunately, emotions are not controlled by our logical left brain. They are a right brain response to what happens to us and not governed by reason. When somebody we love leaves us, for *whatever* reason, we are hurt deeply and, so often with hurt, anger lurks beneath the surface. We must recognize anger for what it is and admit it. One of the major reasons people do not get over the loss of a love is because they have either never recognized or have denied their anger and have failed to resolve it.

What can be even harder to recognize and admit for many is anger at God. For some reason or other, it seems to be a human trait to blame God for things that grieve us. It is important to realize that God doesn't get upset with us or love us any the less because we are angry at him.

I have two sons and sometimes they get angry with me (unfortunately it is sometimes with good reason), but I don't love them any less. What I want them to do is to share their feelings with me so we can be close again. God is the same. He knows when we are feeling angry at him and he wants us to tell him so we are no longer at arm's length.

❏ *Second, express your anger creatively.*

Once anger has been recognized, we need to find a way or ways to release it. There are several ways this can be done. One very effective way is to write your feelings out. Remember, it isn't enough to talk about your feelings; you need to feel and experience them in all their intensity.

Write to the person who deserted, divorced, or abandoned you, or who died and left you. Write about all they did to you, how hurt you are, how angry you are at them. Keep writing until all your pent-up feelings are dissipated. Then read the letter out loud, destroy it, and throw it away. You may need to do this a number of times.

Equally as effective is to talk your angry feelings out. Go to a private place where you feel safe and pretend that you are with the person whom you are angry at. Talk to them as if they were with you in the same room or in your car. Yell if you must. Just make sure that what you are saying is connected to what you are feeling.

Go to your bedroom and beat on your pillow. It won't hurt you and it won't hurt the pillow! It is much better to hit things than to take it out on your kids and hit them, or to kick the cat, which often happens when people don't resolve their anger.

Another powerful way to resolve anger is to role-play with a trusted friend or a trained counselor, or in an understanding support-type therapy group. Choose somebody who in any way reminds you of the person you have lost, have them role-play that person, and then speak to them as if they were the person who left you. This is now done in hospitals to help hurting people. Called psychodrama, it is extremely effective and is perhaps one of the most effective ways to deal with pent-up feelings.

❏ *Third, share your anger with God.*

Tell him exactly how you feel. Ask him to give you the insight to recognize your true feelings and the courage to deal with them openly and honestly. Also confess to God any way you may have hurt or wronged the person you have lost and ask him to forgive you. This will clear the way for you to forgive the one who has hurt you.

Once you have dealt with the anger and put that behind you, then either write (again, not necessarily to be sent) to the person you lost, or talk to them as if they were with you, and tell them that you forgive them for leaving and/or for hurting you. Spell out every way they have hurt you and say, "I forgive you for this." Make this forgiveness a conscious choice, an act of your will.

If we fail to resolve our anger and forgive the one who hurt us, we will carry our resentment into every new relationship. Unresolved grudges turn into bitterness which in turn poisons every close relationship. Grudges work like a cancer and can turn into one. Literally. One thing is certain: If we fail to resolve our past we are destined to repeat it. And, if we fail to forgive we will be bound by the past.

Forgiving doesn't mean that you forget the events that hurt. That isn't realistic. To forgive actually means to let loose, to let go. You resolve your anger by expressing it creatively until it is gone. Then you avoid nursing any grudges against the person who hurt you, and you set yourself free from resentment, and get on with the rest of your life. What you forget is not the event, but the *bitterness*.

Remember, too, that forgiveness doesn't require reconciliation. To be reconciled depends on the response of the other person. It's wonderful when it happens, but too often it doesn't. Fortunately, forgiveness depends only on you.

Admitting and resolving your anger and forgiving may not be easy, but it is essential for physical, mental, and spiritual health. It is also essential for healthy new relationships.

A child once explained forgiveness as "the odor that flowers breathe when they are trampled on." Do you feel your heart has been trampled on or crushed through the loss of a love? If so, as you let go of your anger, your life will breathe out a fresh fragrance, too, and enrich every life you touch.

9

Guard against a Rebound

"I'M FALLING IN LOVE AGAIN!"

Exciting, yes. Wise, no. That is, if you're still too close to your loss.

I live close to a high mountain, but I can't see it from where I live. This is because I live *too* close to it. The lower mountains in front of it block my view. To see the highest mountain peak, I have to drive several miles away from it. That puts it in its proper perspective as it towers above the lesser mountains in the foreground.

Life is like that. When we are too close to a painful situation, we often can't see things as they really are. Our perspective is distorted. We need to distance ourselves sufficiently so we can have a clearer picture of ourselves before making any decisions or commitments that will affect the rest of our life.

Falling in love again soon after the loss of a love can be an exhilarating way to fill your nagging emptiness but, if you do this too soon before having resolved your past hurt, you may be leaving yourself open for more hurt.

To avoid further hurt, be aware of and avoid the following pitfalls.

❏ *First, be aware of your vulnerability.*

When you are hurting and lonely, be conscious of how vulnerable you are. It can be very tempting to get involved in another relationship as a means of avoiding the need to deal with your hurt and other painful emotions.

One young woman I know, whose husband had died, fell "madly in love" with and married the first man who came along and made a fuss over her. In her own words, "It was a disaster!" Now she is divorced and has two losses to mourn as she still hasn't faced and resolved the loss of her first husband who died.

Another woman I know, now in her fifties, had a broken heart when she was a teenager and married the first man who took her out. She has lived to regret her decision to marry too soon and now her health has broken.

❏ *Second, know that true love can wait.*

I recently counseled a couple who were planning on getting married. The woman had been married once before, the man several times. They had only been dating a few weeks when they talked about getting married. Less than six weeks later, they were engaged. The man's current divorce wasn't even final and he was rushing into another marriage.

I strongly urged this couple to postpone their marriage and get as much counseling as necessary to ensure that they wouldn't repeat former mistakes. "When the counselor says you are ready to marry, then go ahead," I suggested. Their clergyman felt and advised them the same way.

Our advice was painful but, if heeded, could prove to be extremely valuable for them. They had everything to gain and nothing to lose by waiting and working through unresolved problems from the past. And they had everything to lose if they moved too fast before resolving the issues that caused them to be divorced before. The point is: Love can wait; lust can't. Only love lasts; lust never does.

Happy marriages are
made only
by happy people.

It may not always be so, but past performance is usually an accurate guide to future behavior. Unless people take the time to resolve their past, they are destined to repeat it. Some people are tragedies waiting to happen simply because they won't or don't take the time and make the effort to face themselves and resolve past problems. Instead of doing this, they rush into new relationships and wonder why they keep getting hurt.

❏ *Third, don't be another statistic.*

Statistics remind us that 85 percent of divorced men and 76 percent of divorced women marry again within fourteen months of their divorce. Those who marry again within twelve months or sooner have a 70 percent chance of being divorced again! Even those who wait longer have a 55 percent chance of being divorced again.

There's no need to become a hermit; just be aware of your vulnerability. Strengthen your friendships and socialize. Just don't rush into a commitment with the opposite sex before you have resolved your hurt and have distanced yourself sufficiently from the pain, so you can see things in their proper perspective. Realize that lasting happiness comes from within yourself, not from another person. Happy marriages are made only by happy people.

❏ *Fourth, watch for other excesses.*

Because you are vulnerable, there are other areas you will also need to be on your guard against. For instance, you may be tempted to buy things you can't afford and don't need and get yourself in deep water financially.

Your resistance may be low to the temptation not to take proper care of yourself, not to eat properly, not to get enough rest, to throw discipline to the wind, and to develop or return to bad habits you've struggled with before.

It takes considerable energy to deal with the rush of feelings you are experiencing and the emotional turmoil you are going through. Your resistance is naturally low, so be sure to take care of yourself and guard against excesses. Eat a well-balanced diet, stay away from junk food, get plenty of rest and exercise. Live as balanced a life as possible to help resist those bad habits.

❏ *Fifth, take charge of your emotions.*

Even though your feelings may seem overpowering at times, there's no need to allow them to control you or your behavior. Don't deny your emotions, but say to yourself when you feel like you are going under or out of control, "What would I do if I weren't feeling this way?"

Then act accordingly. This puts you in charge of your emotions and behavior—which, by the way, is another hallmark of emotional maturity.

God has given us a head as well as a heart. It is wise to use both. Even if five years have passed since you were hurt, if you haven't resolved that pain, then any amount of time is too soon to get into another long-term relationship. Take time to heal, to grow, and to become the person God wants you to be.

Seek God's will in all your relationships. Ask for his wisdom and guidance, for he has promised to give wisdom to all who ask for it. God wants what is best for you and for your growth. Commit and trust your life to him every day and await his time.

As the Bible says, "Trust in the Lord with all your heart, and do not rely on your own insight. In all your ways acknowledge him, and he will make straight your paths."

10

Face Loneliness Head-On

"LONELINESS, IT'S SUCH A SAD AFFAIR." Karen Carpenter seemed to echo her own pain in this song she sang so well. It seems her loneliness was so great it consumed her and took her life, for she starved herself to death.

Loneliness is as universal as the common cold and considerably more painful. It can be crippling. It's like reaching out and closing your hand on emptiness, leaving you with a dull, throbbing, endless pain.

Very few ever escape times of loneliness. Even lovers can be lonely. And marriages can fall apart because one or both partners expected the other to take away their loneliness.

Loneliness can be even more intense when you experience the loss of a loved one through death, divorce, separation or rejection. It is not something to be ignored, but to be handled in constructive ways. These guidelines should help.

❏ *First, don't run from your loneliness.*

The first impulse when loneliness strikes is to run from it and fill the empty void with anything that will relieve its throbbing pain. We feel we must avoid it at all costs, not realizing that to do so can be very costly.

Loneliness needs to be felt, accepted, and understood to be resolved, not run away from.

Among the costly ways of running from loneliness are seeking to anesthetize its pain by alcohol or drugs, symbolically sucking in our feelings and trying to blow them away in smoke with tobacco or marijuana, looking for relief through illicit sex fixes, attempting to stuff our empty void with food, seeking to deaden the pain by going on spending sprees, falling madly in love, over-busyness, or anything that stops us facing the real causes of our loneliness.

All of these things may quiet the pain, but none can deaden it. All they do is postpone it and make it more painful somewhere down the line.

Loneliness needs to be felt, accepted, and understood to be resolved, not run away from. Admittedly, it's a lot easier said than done, but loneliness needs to be worked through, not around. To understand it and come to terms with it, we need to feel its intensity. If, however, every time we feel lonely, we run away from it, we will never conquer it. Rather, it will conquer us.

❏ *Second, find peace within yourself.*

If we are single, it is essential that we come to terms with our singleness and find peace within ourselves if we are to find peace with another person. As long as we are dependent on anybody or anything outside ourselves to take away our loneliness, we will neither overcome it nor find true love. Only free people can love freely.

As we allow ourselves to feel our loneliness, we can begin to recognize that intense loneliness is often a symptom of a much deeper loneliness. This deeper loneliness can come from feelings of isolation, alienation, abandonment, rejection, and neglect—or a feeling of not being wanted, nurtured, accepted or adequately loved in childhood. When this is so, present loneliness hooks into the deeper loneliness from the past and amplifies its pain. The present has merely triggered forgotten memories from earlier times. The agony can be severe.

One of the benefits of a broken heart, therefore, is that its loneliness can bring you face to face with these unresolved feelings from the past and give you an opportunity to resolve them. You don't do this by running away from them. If you do, they will drive you to keep running and destine you to keep repeating the same mistakes.

You don't have to keep running. But you do need to allow yourself to feel and face the pain. If you didn't feel adequately loved as a child, admit it and allow yourself to experience the terrible sense of alienation. Only then can you resolve it. Only then can you realize that you are no longer a child and those feelings and fears are no longer relevant to your world of today.

If you don't bring these feelings to consciousness and accept them, you will act them out blindly and may unconsciously set yourself up to be rejected or abandoned again to prove to yourself that your feelings are correct. You may even be irresistibly drawn to a person just like the parent who rejected or hurt you, in an unconscious effort to get the love you never received as a child. That person will just as likely treat you in a similar way and you will be rejected again.

❏ *Third, face the truth.*

In our society, most adults keep living out the programming of their childhood. We change that programming by facing the truth about ourselves.

It was Jesus who gave us the life-changing principle when he said, "You will know the truth and the truth will set you free." Facing the truth about ourselves can be very difficult because we tend to defend against such truth tenaciously. Unless we face the truth, however, we will never be free to change, nor will we ever resolve the pains from the past that drive us unconsciously and cause us to keep repeating our mistakes.

One of the most effective ways I have found to face myself is to begin with praying the right prayer. Many a time I have prayed, "Oh, God, face me with the truth about myself. If possible, do it gently but, if not, don't spare me for my tears. Don't ever let me off the hook. Whatever the cost confront me with my own reality. Let me see myself as you see me."

I have prayed this same prayer in other situations as well, including relationships I have been in. "God," I have prayed, "face me with the truth about this relationship."

Sometimes the answer has been very painful, but I have never ever prayed this prayer without getting a direct answer. In some situations, the answer has come in two weeks. Another time it took two years, but the answer always came. It is one of the most powerful and life-changing prayers I have ever prayed.

But to pray it and get an answer, you have to mean it. To find truth, you have to want it with all your heart and want it so badly that you are willing to pay the price. But truth is the only thing that can set you free from your past.

❏ *Fourth, deal with your present.*

Not all loneliness, of course, is caused by unmet needs from the past. Some is caused by unmet needs in the present—by not having a friend or a sense of belonging to a group of at least one other person. Because "no man is an island," we cannot survive alone.

In his book *The Wounded Healer,* Henri Nouwen wrote:

> A man can keep his sanity and stay alive as long as there is at least one person who is waiting for him. A dying mother can stay alive to see her son before she gives up the struggle; a soldier can prevent his mental and physical disintegration when he knows that his wife and children are waiting for him. But when "nothing and nobody" is waiting, there is no chance to survive in the struggle for life.[1]

Another benefit of loneliness, therefore, is the realization that we need other people and need to make the effort to develop meaningful friendships. The key to succeeding in doing this is to make yourself friendly.

In looking for new friends, go to the right places to meet the kind of people you want to meet. Remember that other people are lonely and are looking for friendships, too. Introduce yourself to others. Take a genuine interest in them. Ask "why" as well as "what" questions so you can get to know them better. Use your telephone. It is a wonderful connection to other people.

Loneliness seen in this light is not something to be feared. Rather, it is a gift, an opportunity for growth and personal enrichment.

Life's deepest satisfactions come from relationships. People obviously need other people. As the old song says, "People who need people are the luckiest people in the world." But we need to be interdependent with and not *over*dependent on them. Being overdependent on other people, activities, or things means we have never come to terms with our sense of aloneness and loneliness from childhood. We are still not at home with ourselves.

Therefore, accept your loneliness as an opportunity to face and resolve your past, to grow until you feel at home with yourself, and thereby strengthen current friendships and develop wholesome new relationships.

11

Get into
a Support Group

"BANK ON PEOPLE, NOT MACHINES," was the campaign slogan of one bank's employees at the time their bank was introducing automatic teller machines.

As helpful as it is, our high-tech society has unfortunately replaced a considerable amount of people contact. This, along with the passing of the extended family, has added to modern man's sense of isolation. Furthermore, the larger the cities we live in, the greater the sense of isolation becomes. You can live in an apartment and rarely even see your neighbors, let alone talk to them, even though their bedroom wall happens to be your bedroom wall, too!

In addition, our society has become very materialistically oriented rather than people oriented—which adds to modern humanity's sense of isolation. Most of us invest years of earnings in houses and cars and endless things, but precious little time, effort, or money in personal growth in order to enrich our personal lives and enhance our inter-personal relationships.

People don't socialize nearly as much as they did in times gone by. Hours of neighborly conversation have yielded to endless hours sitting in non-communicative, passive silence in front of the television screen.

The only person many people have to bare their soul to is their paid psychiatrist.

The more high-tech our society has become, the more we seem to be alienated from one another.

It's not by chance, therefore, that in recent years numerous groups have sprung up where people can hug, cry, and share their feelings in safety and why professional counseling has become a modern phenomenon. Sadly, the only person many people have to bare their soul to is their paid psychiatrist.

If people in general feel a sense of isolation, how much more do those who have lost a loved one through death? Even these people, however, will—for a time at least—generally receive sympathy and support. Before long, though, they will feel very much alone.

But the divorced often feel isolated immediately. Some are even ostracized—by family, former friends, and even their church. Their sense of isolation can be severe. Some people can be very cruel in the way they shoot their wounded; something, hopefully, they wouldn't even do to an enemy.

Broken-hearted, hurting people badly need the support of understanding, non-judgmental friends. One very helpful place to find this type of support is in a small group.

For example, the church that I attend has support-care groups for all ages and for many needs. There are groups for parents of teens, for those caught in substance abuse, for the spouses of alcoholics, for singles, divorced, single parents, teens, and so on. It is important to find the right group. The following tips might help.

❏ *Find a group that meets your needs or start your own.*

One of the best things you can do for yourself when you are going through a time of loss is to find and join a support group that meets your needs—a group where you can find a genuine sense of caring, understanding, acceptance, and belonging.

To find such a group call your church, other churches, your family physician, a trained counselor or social worker, or call the social service or mental health service in the yellow pages of the telephone directory.

If you can't find such a group, start your own. I did about eighteen years ago. I had no idea what I was doing or how to lead such a group, but I found that there were others who wanted to be in a share/support group and we learned as we went. That group stayed together for five years and was a great source of strength for myself and others in it. It helped me through a very difficult time in my life.

❏ *Find a group where you feel safe.*

I am such a strong believer in the small group concept that I have commenced a more in-depth psychodrama support/therapy group in my own home on Thursday nights.

It's for people who have been hurt, who have gone through divorce, or have suffered any kind of loss either as an adult or as a child. It is the most healing group I have ever led or facilitated.

Women who have been raped, women and men who have been sexually abused and have lost their self-respect as a result, divorced people, lonely people—anybody who has experienced any kind of loss as well as people who just want to learn how to communicate their feelings—attend. Here people have a safe place to share their struggles, their failures, their secrets, their tears, and their anger.

There is no judgment, just total acceptance. Here people are learning how to handle their hurts, express their anger, and face the future.

It is very encouraging to see people work through their pain and find a new freedom. One woman who was sexually violated as a child said that, since coming to the group, she has been feeling the best she can remember. For the first time in her life she has found a safe place to deal with her hurt and pain.

I grew up in the church and am now the director of a church service-and-outreach organization. For many years I have searched for what I believed the church should be: a hospital for the healing of hurting people, a place of refuge for the weary, a place of forgiveness for sinners, a place of safety where you could confess your sins and failures without fear of being judged, a place where you could learn about life, a place where you could find healing from the hurts of childhood and life, a place where you could be open and honest.

I never found it in years of education or theological training. I never found it in books or in a church building. I found it, finally, in my own living room, weeping with those who weep and sharing with those who share. This is what the real church is all about.

I strongly urge you to find such a church or such a group or start your own. If you would like some tips on how to start such a group, write to the address listed in the preface.

Just don't bear your burden alone. Get into a group where you can find acceptance, a sense of belonging, and the support you need to help you grow and heal your broken heart.

❏ *Don't forget to hold hands.*

Some time ago, I read the following article by Robert Fulghum from his book, *All I Really Need to Know I Learned in Kindergarten.* It's priceless advice:

> All I really need to know about life I learned in kindergarten. Wisdom was not at the tip of the graduate school mountain, but here in the sandbox at nursery school.
>
> These are the things I learned: Share everything. Play fair. Don't hit people. Put things back where you found them. Clean up your own mess. Don't take things that aren't yours. Say you're sorry when you hurt somebody. Wash your hands before you eat. Flush! Warm cookies and cold milk are good for you. Live a balanced life. Learn and think, draw and paint, sing and dance, play and work a little every day.
>
> Take a nap every afternoon. When you get out into the world, watch for traffic, hold hands and stick together. Be aware of wonder. Remember the little seed in the plastic cup. The roots go down and the plant goes up and nobody really knows how or why, but we are all like that.
>
> Goldfish, hamsters, white mice and even the little seed in the plastic cup—they all die. So do we.
>
> And then remember the Dick-and-Jane books, and the first word you learned—the biggest word of all—*Look.*
>
> Everything you need to know is in there somewhere. The Golden Rule, love and basic sanitation; ecology, politics and sane living.

Think of what a better world it would be if all of us—the whole world—had cookies and milk about three o'clock every afternoon and then lay down with our blankets for a nap! Or if we had a basic policy in our nation (and other nations) always to put things back where we found them and to clean up our own mess.

And it's still true, no matter how old you are, that when you go out into the world, it's best to hold hands and stick together.[2]

I had a friend whom I met in kindergarten. We went through school, technical college, and national service together and, even though later we lived thousands of miles apart, we never lost contact with each other.

Recently my friend fell on hard times, suffered a great loss, became discouraged, withdrew into himself, and took his life. A tragic waste. How sad it is when, in our hour of deepest need, as adults we forget to hold hands.

12

Be Committed
to Personal Growth

WHY IS IT THAT THE DAUGHTER of an alcoholic is often attracted to and marries a man who also becomes an alcoholic or develops a related dependency problem? Why is it that the son of a domineering, controlling mother often falls in love with the same kind of woman?

Why is it that a compliant, submissive woman marries a domineering man? Or a weak, passive male marries a dominant woman? And why does a man who felt abandoned as a child marry four women who all abandon him?

Or why does a woman who was physically abused as a child marry a man who physically abuses her? And if I complain that my spouse has a serious weakness or problem, why was I attracted to this person in the first place?

These things don't happen by chance; there's always a reason. The way we select marriage partners in Western society is highly suspect. The staggering divorce rate attests to the fact that our system is not working too well. One reason is that we are attracted to the person where, among other things, our neuroses (unresolved problems and unmet needs from the past) mesh and we call it "love"! In other words, much of what we call love is an overdependent need.

---

*The person who was
deeply hurt in childhood
and is afraid to love will
often marry another person
who is afraid to love and
end up living unhappily
together apart.*

For example, sometimes without realizing it we are attracted to and marry a person just like the parent whose love we didn't receive as a child, especially the parent of the opposite sex. This is because we are used to that kind of relationship and it is often an unconscious attempt to gain our lost childhood love from the parent whose love we felt we never received. In other words, we marry a substitute mother or father. It doesn't and cannot work.

Another example is that a domineering man is not usually attracted to a domineering woman or vice-versa. Domineering people only feel comfortable with someone they can control. This is why they are attracted to someone passive and overdependent.

Likewise, the overdependent person needs someone he or she can lean on, so they are attracted to a partner who is controlling and domineering. Or the person who was deeply hurt in childhood and is afraid to love will often marry another person who is afraid to love and end up living unhappily together apart.

The person who needs someone to depend upon them is usually attracted to a needy overdependent person, because they only feel loved if they are needed and have someone "to fix."

The tragedy is that the irresistible attraction that magnetically draws us together, if not faced and resolved, often ends up driving us apart!

If, therefore, we are suffering loss through a broken relationship or divorce, the critical issue is that we take a good, hard *honest* look at ourselves to see why we married or got involved with the type of person we did. No matter what our partner did, we, too, always contributed something.

One of the most difficult things for us to do is to be honest with ourselves and see what we contributed. If we aren't, we are bound to keep repeating the same mistakes because the relational games we play always follow the way we were programmed.

Another benefit, therefore, of a broken heart is that, if we are wise, we will allow the pain to bring us to the point where we are willing to look honestly at ourselves and do something about resolving our past. Doing this can change our whole lives. Chances are we will never have a better opportunity to grow than we do right now.

Unfortunately, most people would rather find another partner as soon as possible or do anything to quiet their pain instead of taking time out to work on their personal growth before making a commitment to another person. Don't let this happen to you. Let your pain be the motivating force to help you grow and become a much better, wiser, and more mature and loving person.

The painful truth is that we are as sick as our relationships and end up with the person we deserve! This is why, if we want healthy relationships, we need to be healthy ourselves and why it is so important to become the right person. Only then will we find the right partner.

Becoming the right person comes only through recovery and through personal growth, and these take genuine commitment to each of the following.

❏ *First, a commitment to wholeness.*

Jesus Christ was the master healer. On one occasion he approached a man who had been crippled for thirty-eight years! It's hard to believe the question Jesus asked this man. He said, "Do you want to be made whole?" Could you imagine anybody who had been handicapped for thirty-eight years *not* wanting to be made whole?

Unfortunately, some people don't want to get well. They prefer to stay as they are in order to get sympathy or attention, to avoid personal responsibility or to have somebody else take care of them. Others only want to get well if the doctor or counselor will make them well without any real effort or cost on their part. According to people in the health-care professions, only a small percentage of people are prepared to pay the cost and do whatever it takes to get well. Dr. Bernie S. Siegel, author of *Love, Medicine and Miracles,* comments:

> About fifteen to twenty percent of all patients unconsciously, or even consciously, wish to die. On some level, they welcome cancer or another serious illness as a way to escape their problems through death or disease. These are the patients

who show no signs of stress when they find out their diagnosis. As the doctor is struggling to get them well, they are resisting and trying to die. If you ask them how they are they say, "Fine." And what is troubling them? "Nothing."[3]

Siegel goes on to say that the majority of patients—about 60 to 70 percent—are like actors auditioning for a part. They act according to the doctor's wishes . . . take their medicine and so on, but rely wholly on the doctor to make them better. Given a choice, they would rather be operated on than actively participate in their own healing and well-being.

The people who genuinely want to get better are only 15 to 20 percent of patients. These are the ones who refuse to play the victim. They accept full responsibility for their healing and do everything that is needed to recover. They are truly committed.

Doctors Frank Minirth and Paul Meier of the Minirth-Meier counseling clinic give similar figures. They say the following:

> People are afraid of the truth. We once asked our staff of counselors to estimate how many of their patients come to our clinic to learn the truth about themselves so that they can do something to correct whatever is wrong. The therapist's best guesstimate was that only twenty-five percent of all [their] clients want to find out the truth and even fewer want to deal with it.
>
> Most patients visit the clinic looking for quick and easy solutions. They want a pill to make their anxiety go away. Or they want a counselor to listen to their problems and then blame the problems on someone else. The last thing a patient wants to hear is that his own anger or guilt or jealousy is the source of his anxiety and that he is responsible for getting rid of the negative emotion.[4]

As Jesus said to the crippled man, "Do you want to be made whole?" Only those who are genuinely committed to growth and accept total responsibility for their growth will ever find wholeness. What they actually do, not what they say they want, tells how genuine they are in their commitment to growth.

❏ *Second, a commitment to truth.*

One of the most difficult things in life is to be honest with ourselves. To some degree or another we have all been hurt, we have all failed and made mistakes, we have all sinned and we all have personal weaknesses, pockets of immaturity and areas of insecurity. We are afraid that, if we get found out we won't be liked, so—like Adam, the first man to sin—we hide.

We hide our real selves from God because we are afraid of his rejection. We also hide our real selves from other people and pretend to be something that we aren't for fear of rejection from the people we need to love us. When we do this for long enough, we eventually hide from ourselves so we no longer know who or what we really are. At the point of hiding from ourselves, if it could be measured, we begin to die as growing persons.

The only way we ever grow is to come out of hiding and quit the pretense of acting like somebody we are not. As long as we pretend, we can never change, because we fail to see the need to change. We are also too intent on keeping up the false front and mask.

It can be very scary to come out of hiding, but it is the only way to grow and be made whole. Before we can ever change what we are, we need to see and admit what we are. Being truthful with ourselves is thus the beginning of the process of all personal growth. It is the only road to the healing of persons.

As Jesus said: "You will know the truth, and the truth will set you free."

❑ *Third, a commitment to integrity.*

Integrity is keeping your word, doing what you say you are going to do. Keeping the commitments you make. Being true to yourself and your convictions. It is standing up for what you know to be right whatever the cost. It is admitting and putting things right when you have failed. It is establishing wholesome values and living consistently with them.

Maintaining personal integrity is essential for personal growth and wholeness.

❑ *Fourth, a commitment to personal responsibility.*

We will deal more with responsibility in a later chapter, but let us mention here that the acceptance of personal responsibility is absolutely essential for personal growth. As long as I blame anybody else for my problems and the difficulties I have, I will never resolve them. People only hurt me, control me, make me feel angry and so on if I allow them to.

While others are responsible for what *they* do, I am totally responsible for how I react, how I feel and for what *I* do. I am also totally responsible for my own personal growth, for what I do about resolving my hurts and my past. Nobody else can or will do it for me. I and I alone, with the help of God, am the only one who can make me grow.

❑ *Fifth, a commitment to persistence.*

The level of pain of the people who are in our support-growth-healing group is almost hard to believe. Things that people have had done to them, often as infants when they weren't responsible at all, are tragic. They have been sexually abused by fathers and friends and they have been neglected and physically abused by insensitive and hostile parents. Some of the things people have done to them when they were children are positively sickening.

As adults, some have been raped, deserted, betrayed and divorced, or are still in abusive relationships. Some come for a little while, but drop out without ever having resolved their pain. The ones who are finding growth and healing are the ones who admit their problems, keep their word and their commitments and thereby maintain integrity.

They are the ones who accept total responsibility for their own recovery and total well-being. They are the ones who are persistent. They keep coming and they keep working on their issues.

They are the ones who want to be made whole. The half-hearted never make it. The price is too high.

You can resolve your past. You can overcome your loss. You can change your life. You can become the person God wants you to be. You can develop your total potential. You can find fulfillment in your personal life and relationships. You can have new dreams and new goals. But to find and achieve these takes commitment: real commitment to wholeness, to truth, to integrity, to recovery, to personal responsibility, and to persistence.

And that's the decision and choice only you can make. It's yours for the asking.

13

Realize That Failure Is Never Final

DID YOU KNOW THAT Walt Disney went broke seven times and had a nervous breakdown before he became successful? And did you realize that Enrico Caruso failed so many times trying to reach his high notes that his voice teacher told him to quit singing? Were you aware that Thomas Edison failed over six thousand times before perfecting the electric light-bulb?

But did these men really fail? On one occasion, a young newspaper journalist told Edison that his plan would never work because gas lighting was "here to stay." He also wanted to know why Edison kept on trying when he kept failing so many times.

"Young man," Edison replied, "I have not failed. I have successfully discovered six thousand ways that won't work."

April 7 or any other day may have been the final day of your divorce, the day you were rejected or the day you lost or buried a loved one, but remember that April 8 was the first day of the rest of your life. It was a day of new beginnings. If you haven't done your grieving, do it now. Face, accept and resolve your pain, get up even if you have to drag yourself up, and go on. To do this effectively, there are several valuable qualities we need to have.

Failure is an event, never a person.

❏ *First, have the right attitude.*

Attitude is what makes the difference between a painful experience becoming a failure or a success. It has been said that there are three reactions we can have towards a failure or mistake. We can resolve never to make a mistake again— a noble ideal, but totally unrealistic. We can let the failure leave us timid and afraid to step out again for fear of being hurt again; that is soul-destroying. Or we can determine that our failure will be our teacher and so gain from the experience. It has also been said that if we fail to heed the teachings of failure, we will never hear the voice of success.

A favorite story of mine is told about three stone cutters all working together in the same place chipping away at building blocks. When asked what he was doing, the first man replied, "I'm cutting stones in order to make a living." When the second stonemason was asked, "What are you doing?," he answered by holding up one of the stones. "I'm forming building bricks by cutting them exactly the size and shape they are supposed to be," he replied. The answer by the third stonecutter was something else. He said, "I'm building a cathedral."

Life is what we make of it. We see what we choose to see, believe what we want to believe and get out of it what we put into it. It's our attitude that makes the difference.

We can allow our failures to hurt us or help us. We can see them as a disaster or we can see them as one of the most valuable experiences we can ever have. True, we need mountaintop experiences from time to time to give us encouragement, but we don't grow through these. We don't look at ourselves with an eye to improvement when everything is going right either. It is in the valley of our disappointments and through our failures that we are given the opportunity to take stock of our lives and move towards a greater level of growth and maturity.

Emmett Miller in his article "In Helping Others to Succeed" put it this way: "Oftentimes, failure can be a creative experience in disguise. Indeed, perhaps one of the most powerful ways to look at failure is to see it as a creative experience attempting to emerge. What you are calling a mistake is, in fact, an attempt by the deeper levels of the mind to find a better solution."[5]

❏ *Second, know what your purpose in life is.*

Another effective way to turn failure into success and overcome heartbreaking situations is to know what your purpose in life is. The more clearly defined that purpose is and the more deeply it is embedded in your conscious and unconscious mind, the less failures will set you back.

A spacecraft enroute to the moon is off course 90 percent of the time. It's pulled back by the earth's gravity. It's continually drawn to one side or the other by other forces. But it has a built-in computer that has a singleness of purpose that homes in on the moon. The computer is making continual corrections to keep the spacecraft on target with its purpose and goal.

Life's like that. There is no defeat except from within, no really insurmountable barrier save our own inherent weakness of purpose. If our eye is on our goal, if we have a singleness of purpose, nothing will stop us getting to where we are going.

❏ *Third, remember that failure is an event, not a person.*

Just because you may have failed in your marriage, in another relationship or other situation doesn't mean that you are a failure as a person. Not at all. Realize that the only real failure is not to try, or not to keep on trying, or not to get up one more time than you've been knocked down. The important thing is to learn from your past, to use it as an opportunity to grow and to get up and move ahead.

❏ *Fourth, give God a chance.*

If you feel like you have failed, seriously consider giving God a chance. If you believe you've done wrong, ask him to forgive you and be sure to forgive yourself. Then turn your failure into a valuable learning experience, a stepping stone toward a better you.

In his book, *Beginning Again,* Terry Hershey writes:

God not only says that failure is never the final word, but that your area of weakness will become your area of strength. Where you were weak and learned grace will become a place where you can reach out and touch the lives of others who need the same good news. That may sound impossible at this point. And that's okay. But the truth remains. God is not only working to heal you, but to heal others through you, to make you what Henri Nouwen called a "wounded healer."[6]

Nouwen explains it this way:

> A deep understanding of his own pain makes it possible for
> [the hurting person] to convert his weakness into strength
> and to offer his own experience as a source of healing to those
> who are often lost in the darkness of their own misunder-
> stood sufferings. Once the pain is accepted and understood,
> a denial is no longer necessary and ministry [to others] can
> become a healing service.[7]

I believe it was Ernest Hemingway who first used the
phrase, "growing strong in the broken places." The idea
behind these words is that where a bone is broken and heals,
it becomes the strongest part of the bone.

The same is true of our broken places—where we have
been hurt, have fallen and failed, or are afraid. When we bring
these to God for his healing, his strength is made perfect
through our weaknesses. This is certainly true in helping
other people. They are helped not through our brilliant logic
or persuasive speech, but through the sharing of our struggles, disappointments, and losses and how, with God's help,
we have overcome. It is a case of one beggar who has found
bread showing other beggars where they can find bread, too.

Thank God for what God wants to teach you through
your failure and what he wants to make out of your life as a
result.

Ralph Waldo Emerson said, "Though we may search the
world over for the beautiful, we find it within or we find it not."

It is from within that God wants to change us. He wants
to transform us from the inside out. Failure presents one of
the best opportunities for God to do this for us and to make
something beautiful out of our life.

As someone else has wisely said, "Success [more often
than not] is failure turned inside out."

14

Discipline Your Thinking

LAST NIGHT, WHEN I WAS TUCKING my young son into bed, he said to me, "What if I can't go to sleep?"

"You will," I replied.

"But what if I can't?" he kept repeating.

"You've never ever had a night when you didn't go to sleep," I said, "but if you keep telling yourself that you can't go to sleep, you will make it very difficult to get to sleep." That seemed to satisfy him. In no time he was sound asleep.

"Men are disturbed," said Epictetus, "not by things, but by the view they take of them." It's how we perceive things and what we keep telling ourselves in our self talk, that either disturbs us or sets us free.

Self talk is what we are thinking about. It is the non-stop dialogue we have with ourselves in our head. According to psychologist David Stoop, author of *Self Talk: Key to Personal Growth,* studies show that we talk to ourselves all of the time . . . at the rate of 1300 words per minute![8]

Our self talk, as well as our beliefs about ourselves, has a profound effect on how we feel and how we act. What we keep telling ourselves about ourselves we eventually believe, and what we believe becomes our reality and self-fulfilling prophecy—what we believe we make happen. Our self talk or thought life is where we either win or lose control of our life.

To take charge of our life we need to take charge of our self talk. We can do this in the following ways.

❏ *First, realize the power of your self talk.*

What we think we either are or will become.

What we keep thinking about affects our emotions as well as our behavior. This is because what the mind dwells on the emotions respond to and the body acts on—for good or bad. For example, if I keep telling myself that I can't live without the person I have lost, I will believe that, act accordingly, and keep myself depressed. As difficult as it may seem, the truth is I *can* live without this person. My mind may resist accepting this fact but, if I keep telling myself this is true, in time I will believe it and recover.

We've all met people who were divorced or lost a loved one years ago and still haven't recovered. One reason is they keep telling themselves they will never get over their loss, so they don't. Their self talk makes it so. The opposite is also true. People who tell themselves they can recover from their loss, do. Their self talk also makes it so.

Temptation works the same way. Something triggers a thought in our mind and we keep dwelling on it. The more we think about it, the more we want it; the more we want it, the more our emotions get hooked into it; and the more we feel about it, the bigger it grows until it becomes larger than life. Eventually we act out our thoughts and feelings and give in to the temptation.

What the mind dwells on, the body will act on.

Temptation always starts in the mind. Doing good operates the same way. It, too, starts with our thoughts and self talk.

Our self talk also strongly affects our moods. For example, if we concentrate on negative thoughts, we are likely to have negative feelings. If we concentrate on depressing thoughts, we reinforce depressing feelings. On the other hand, if we concentrate on positive thoughts, we are likely to have positive feelings.

❏ *Second, think realistically as well as positively.*

Positive thinking is essential for taking charge of your life, but it also needs to be realistic. For instance, if you have unresolved grief or anger or unmet needs, no amount of "positive thinking," if it denies the reality of these feelings and needs, will take away the pain and hurt. It will only bury them and make them worse later on.

The realistic, positive way to think is: "Yes, I am hurting. I need to resolve my feelings of hurt and anger and make sure I get my needs met in legitimate ways so I can think straight again."

It's useless to tell a starving man not to think about food so he will feel better. If you work hard enough on his thinking, you might succeed in getting him to feel better—just before he dies. It is also ill-advised to tell a friend who has just lost a loved one through death or divorce not to think about it and not to feel bad. There are times when we ought to feel bad. To deny these feelings is to push them below the level of consciousness and have them erupt in damaging ways later on.

Furthermore, if our needs for friendship, love, sense of belonging and many other valid needs are not met, no amount of positive thinking will take away the thoughts and feelings of loneliness, emptiness and so on. The positive thing to do is to acknowledge these needs and get them met in positive ways.

❏ *Third, choose your thoughts carefully.*

Mark Twain said, "People in general are about as happy as they make up their minds to be." And Marcus Antoninus said, "No man is happy who does not think himself so." Like temptation, peace and happiness begin in the mind.

There are many things and circumstances in life that we have little or no control over, but we do have control of our thoughts. The sooner we realize this and choose our thoughts carefully, the sooner we will change our whole outlook on life. By carefully choosing and controlling our thoughts, we take charge of our lives.

When we are hurting, we tend to give in to negative thoughts. And when we have been deserted and our self-image has taken a blow, we tend to think the worst. At these times, we need to choose and guard our thoughts even more carefully.

❏ *Fourth, focus your thoughts on the person you want to be.*

Fortunately, the mind can concentrate only on one thought at a time and we can choose what that thought will be. Because of this and because what we keep thinking about affects how we feel and what we do, we need to focus our thoughts on the person we want to become.

For example, if you are feeling very insecure because of your loss (which is often the case), one of the most effective ways to build up your self-esteem and feel good about yourself is to focus on the following thought and keep repeating it to yourself: "God loves me so I love me. God loves me so I love me. God loves me so I love me." By saying this to yourself, it can become a part of your belief system.

Another constructive way to rebuild a shattered self-image is to make a point of thanking God for all the good things in your life and think about these. The apostle Paul says, "Whatever is true, whatever is noble, whatever is right, whatever is pure, whatever is lovely, whatever is admirable—if anything is excellent or praiseworthy—think about such things." By doing this, we can take charge of and change our life by taking charge of our thinking.

If you keep telling yourself in your mind that you will never get over your hurt, that you will never amount to anything, that you will never get better, you won't. But if you keep telling yourself that you are on the road to recovery, that you will get over your hurt, that you are becoming a much better and more loving person, you will. Your concentrated thoughts will be your self-fulfilling prophecy.

If you want to take charge of your life, recognize the power of self talk for good or evil, then choose your thoughts carefully, think realistically as well as positively and concentrate your thoughts on the person you want to be.

We are not what we think we are. But what we think . . . we are. As Earl Nightingale put it, "We become what we think about." Or, in the forcible language of Scripture, "As a man thinks in his heart, so is he."

15

Do Something
for Someone Else

I HAD SET ASIDE this afternoon to work on this book but, when I sat down at my desk to write, nothing would come. I had a frustrating writer's block. No way did I feel like writing. I wanted to get on the phone and talk to a friend, work in my garden, take a nap since I could hardly keep my eyes open—do just about anything but write.

But I kept with it and stuck to it. Eventually I broke out of the bind I was in and wrote much of this chapter and the next. Perseverance paid off. The sense of accomplishment made me feel much better than I did a few hours before.

The point I am making is that feelings are not only affected by what we think, but also by what we do. However, as a general rule it is much easier and quicker to *act* our way into *feeling* positive than it is to *feel* our way into *acting* positive. Furthermore, it is probably easier to act our way into feeling good than it is to think our way into it.

If we want to feel good, we need to learn to act the way we want to feel. Or, as the AA people say, "Fake it till you make it." This is not to deny your feelings, but to choose not to let them control you or your actions.

The following suggestions can help you act your way into feeling good.

To ease another's heartache is to forget one's own.

❑ *First, choose how you are going to act.*

As earlier suggested, a very helpful question to ask yourself when you are feeling down, hurt, angry, or have a mental block is this: "What would I do if I weren't feeling this way?" Then do that. This puts you in charge of your feelings and your actions. It doesn't deny your emotions, which is a dangerous path to follow; rather, it acknowledges them, but doesn't allow them to control you.

This is another high mark of maturity. It is also a mark of intelligence. As Brian Tracy says, "If we do intelligent things, we are intelligent. If we do dumb things, we are . . . !"

With practice we can learn to change our feelings by what we do. True, pent-up feelings need to be expressed in creative ways. When we do this and keep doing the right thing, eventually our feelings will catch up with our actions and we will learn to feel good again.

An inquiring person once asked Pascal, "I wish I had your creed so I could live your kind of life." To which Pascal replied, "Start living my kind of life and you will soon have my creed."

❏ *Second, reach out and touch someone.*

Another important thing to do, or rather not to do when you are going through a heartbreaking experience, is to get caught up in feeling sorry for yourself. Those thoughts feed on themselves and very quickly drive you down into a deeper spiral of despair. At times like this you need to get outside of yourself and do something for somebody else.

I shall never forget my maternal grandmother. She lived to be ninety. My grandfather died many years earlier, but my grandmother never sat around feeling sorry for herself. She kept very much alive, happy, healthy, and fulfilled by doing hospital visitation and bringing joy and encouragement to the sick.

When you are feeling blue or to help yourself not to feel blue, make a habit of reaching out each day and doing something helpful for somebody else—even if it is just speaking a kind word, making a phone call, sending a greeting card, or writing a note to tell somebody you are thinking about them.

Remember the words of Jesus:"If you give, you will get! Your gift will return to you in full and overflowing measure, pressed down, shaken together to make room for more and running over. Whatever measure you use to give—large or small—will be used to measure what is given back to you."

The fact is you can get without giving, but you cannot give without getting. If, therefore, you want to feel better, do something helpful for somebody else.

There is a story of two women who lived in a convalescent center. Both had suffered serious strokes. Margaret's left side had been left restricted, while Ruth's right side was affected. Both ladies had been accomplished pianists but had given up hope of ever playing again. The director of the center suggested to them that they try playing the piano together. They did and succeeded. They played excellent music and, better still, developed a beautiful friendship.

Three thousand years ago, Solomon wrote: "Two are better than one, because they have a good return for their work: If one falls down, his friend can help him up. But pity the man who falls and has no one to help him up! Also, if two lie down together, they will keep warm. But how can one keep warm alone?"

We need each other and the security that comes from being deeply loved and cared for. But we also need to give love and show care—by loving actions and practical support, spending time with people for their own sake, not just for what we can derive from the relationship.

Thoughtfulness does not come naturally; it is an acquired habit that comes from weeks, months, years of giving, not just taking. Happy is the person who becomes that sort of friend!

16

Do Something for Yourself

IONA MCLAUGHLIN STRUGGLED valiantly to regain meaning and purpose in her life following horrible tragedy. First, she lost her fourteen-year-old daughter, Jane, to a brain tumor. A few days later, her husband Pete and ten-year-old son Jack were killed in an accident which came very close to killing Iona as well.

For months Iona lay in a hospital 1,500 miles away from her home, suffering from the loss of her husband and children and recovering from her painful wounds. What compounded her problem was that she needed to be heavily sedated to sleep at night and became addicted to the drugs the hospital gave her. This presented her with an additional problem to overcome.

When Iona eventually got out of the hospital, she had to face the reality of her life without her husband of twenty years and her two children. One can only imagine the despair she faced as she tried to cope with her loss and adjust to the change from being a wife and mother to being single and childless.

She decided to better herself by going back to school and furthering her education. While there, the cynicism of younger students caused her to question her faith. Maybe the universe was without reason or plan. Her anguish led to thoughts of suicide.

Her question
"Why did it happen?"
changed to
"What do I do now?"

Next, Iona battled with the question, "Why?" At this point, it was a letter from her late husband's father which helped her the most: "God is as sad over this as you are. It is *not* God's will that such things happen. Amid the many circumstances of life, some things happen because we belong to a human society. But God's will is for life to be lived to its fullest. When it isn't, God stands as of old, weeping with us. We believe in immortality. Whatever is commenced here will be completed there. Nothing is lost out of God's care."

Eventually Iona's faith returned. Her question "Why did it happen?" changed to "What do I do now?"

She returned to work by teaching at university level, and, after wrestling with the difficult decision to risk again, eventually remarried. This gave her instant children and grandchildren and considerable fulfillment. She found additional satisfaction as a lecturer, retreat leader, and church member.

Through her deep trials, God taught Iona many lessons about life so she was better able to help other people. Through her determination, she made the opportunity to better qualify herself to do the things she wanted to do. With God's help and her perseverance, she was able to make a new life for herself.[9] If you keep the following in mind, it will help you do the same.

❏ *First, never give up.*

I have read that on one occasion Winston Churchill was asked to address the assembly at the boys school which he had attended. His address went like this:

> Boys, never give up.
> Never, never, never give up!

That was his entire speech—and I'm sure that none of those boys ever forgot that message as long as they lived. I wasn't there, but I don't think I'll ever forget it either and I hope you won't. With worthwhile goals, this attitude can pay great dividends.

Popular author, psychologist, and lecturer, Wayne Dwyer, was unheard of a few years ago. However, he believed in his philosophy of life, quit a very secure university teaching position, wrote a book about it, and bought the entire first printing himself. He then spent two years traveling throughout the entire country giving away his books and getting himself interviewed on every radio and talk show he could find in every city, large and small, and in every country town, large and small. He simply never gave up. He did what he had to do to win. Today he travels the world lecturing.

Today I had lunch with a woman whom I shall call Pattie J. Several years ago, as she was sitting talking to her husband, without any warning whatsoever he had a sudden heart attack and died instantly. Pattie was left to raise four small children. "The only thing I could think of," Pattie told me, "was to find myself another husband as quickly as possible to help raise my children."

Pattie rushed into another marriage far too soon and paid a high price. "It was a disaster," she said. But she hasn't given up. She has learned some very hard lessons, but is now determined with God's help to make something worthwhile out of her life. She got into counseling to work through her losses, is well on the road to recovery, and is now planning to get further training to become qualified for what she wants to do.

❏ *Second, turn your lemon into lemonade.*

Iona McLaughlin didn't allow her losses to embitter or defeat her. Neither has Pattie J. Though the road to recovery was not easy, both took the lemons they were handed and turned them into lemonade. With faith, persistence, and hard work, they turned their tragedies into triumphs.

No matter what happens to us, it is what we choose to do about it that will govern the outcome. As Brian Tracy puts it, "It is choice, not chance, that determines our destiny."

❏ *Third, improve yourself.*

With faith, persistence, and hard work you can turn your tragedy into triumph, too. You can do this by making your time of sadness a time to improve yourself and do something creative.

Work in your garden, plant a tree, do some woodwork, write a poem, read some good books. Do *something* constructive each day.

Redefine your life purpose and establish some new and meaningful goals. Further your education and take that course you've been talking about taking for a long time. Make the opportunity to better qualify yourself to do what you want to do.

Start that business venture you've been wanting to start for years. Begin part-time to get it established. Take some seminars and join a support group to help with your personal growth.

Above all, take time every day to improve the quality of your spiritual life and get close to God. Any or all of these strategies will help rebuild your confidence and assist you to feel much better about yourself. Put together, they will give you a new focus outside of yourself and help you turn your tragedy into a new opportunity.

17
Take Care
of Your Health

THE MOST STRESSFUL EXPERIENCE a person will endure, according to counselors, is the loss of a loved one through death. Divorce is the next most stressful.

It is important at these and other times of high stress that you guard as much as possible against other stressful situations. Now is not the best time to change jobs, go on a crash diet, or go on wild spending sprees buying those things you don't need or can't afford.

Besides avoiding unnecessary stress, it is very important to take proper care of your physical and mental health.

❏ *First, watch your diet.*

Unfortunately, when under stress people tend to eat junk food and neglect their physical health. They end up feeling worse. So make the effort and be sure to eat balanced meals with sufficient fiber, and avoid fatty foods, white sugar and too much salt.

Dr. Melba Colgrove, Dr. Harold H. Bloomfield, and Peter McWilliams in their book, *How to Survive the Loss of a Love,* give the following advice for times of loss:

> Increase the amount of protein you eat. Protein includes meat, fish, fowl, milk, eggs, nuts, seeds, soybeans and whole grains.
>
> Decrease junk foods.
>
> Take a B-vitamin supplement, a C-vitamin supplement, and a multi-vitamin or mineral supplement . . .
>
> Increase calcium (take calcium tablets or, better still, drink more milk) and potassium (again in tablets, or by eating baked potatoes, parsley or bananas).
>
> And . . . eat something every day from each of the four major food groups: meat and poultry, dairy products, fruits and vegetables, breads and cereals.[10]

❏ *Second, exercise regularly.*

Even at the best of times, it is essential to exercise regularly. It is even more important during times of stress, sadness, loneliness and depression. Upset emotions upset the body's chemical balance, and, if left unresolved for too long, impede the body's immune system. Sickness results.

An immediate answer is regular aerobic or other vigorous exercise. This type of exercise burns up excess chemicals such as too much adrenalin and helps bring healing to the body and mind. At the same time, vigorous exercise produces the chemical endorphin which is secreted in the brain and provides a pain-relieving effect like that of morphine.

On more than one occasion when I have been feeling lonely or down, I have fought the temptation to give in to my emotions by withdrawing or trying to sleep it off (which doesn't work anyhow). Instead, I have cycled and hiked to the top of one of the mountains near where I live. I have consistently found that by the time I return after two or more hours of this vigorous workout, my whole mood and attitude is transformed.

The loss of a loved one through death is the most stressful experience a person will endure. Divorce is the next most stressful.

In fact, I have benefited so much from this exercise physically, mentally, and spiritually. I cycle in the foothills regularly through the week and hike and cycle up into the mountains almost every weekend. For those who question how I do this, I have an 18-speed mountain bike and ride up a dirt firetrail. It sure is fun coming down, even if it feels like I'm riding a jack hammer!

Reaching the top of the mountain also became a symbol for me. I kept saying to myself, "I will conquer this mountain, and with God's help I will conquer my fears and loneliness."

And I did. You can, too. With God's help, faith and persistence you can go through your valley of despair and loneliness and conquer every mountain before you. Regular, vigorous exercise is one of the disciplines that will help get you there a little bit sooner . . . and in much better shape, I might add!

❏ *Third, get sufficient rest.*

Any major wound is physically exhausting. Wounds of the heart are no exception. They are even more draining on our energy—emotionally as well as physically. Therefore, make certain you get the extra rest and sleep your body needs at such a time.

None of these needs to be overdone. Moderation and balance are the key words. Just be conscious of the fact that your natural resistance to other ills will be weakened because of the high energy drain used in the emotional healing process.

❏ *Fourth, deal creatively with your emotions.*

As noted earlier, do your grieving now. The less you bottle up your emotions and the more you express them in healthy ways, the less likely you are to suffer physical symptoms. So be sure to keep short accounts of your painful feelings.

I heard of one man just this week who has been going through a very stressful time, a man who keeps all his feelings bottled up inside of himself. He had just found out that he has a cancerous tumor right inside his heart. Symbolically, turning his pain in on himself he is eating his heart out.

As the writer of Proverbs said, "A cheerful heart does good like medicine, but a broken spirit makes one sick." To keep as cheerful a heart as possible, be sure to take good care of your physical health and don't bottle up your emotions.

18

Be a Responsibility Thinker

I'D HAD A VERY BUSY WEEKEND and had barely arrived home late Sunday night when my telephone rang. "Is it convenient for you to talk now?" an all too familiar voice asked.

"No, I'm afraid it's not," I replied. "I'm exhausted and need to get to bed. Can you call back tomorrow?"

But the man didn't stop talking. He began to pour out a tale of woe. He'd already called me several times and once again was telling me how badly his parents were treating him. He blamed them for it all, even though he was a grown man.

Finally I interrupted and said, "Peter, what your parents have done may be terrible, but as long as you keep blaming them or anybody else for your reactions and your present difficulties, you will never get better. I know you want them to change, but you can't do that. If you try to, chances are they will only get more angry at you. The only person any one of us can ever change is ourself."

But Peter was persistent. He wanted me to give him a way to get his parents to change. I couldn't and, even if I could, I wouldn't. Peter will never get better until he accepts full responsibility for changing himself and for what he is going to do about resolving his problems. Nobody else can do these for him! He went away sad.

Admittedly, Peter's case was somewhat extreme, but it does illustrate a very common relationship problem. In a more subtle but just as real way, this is seen in a friend's marriage which is in trouble and the husband writes and asks me to pray for his wife. "She really needs prayer for her problem," he says, but says nothing about *his* problem.

Compare the difference with the woman whose husband has been unfaithful to her once too often. She has put her foot down, separated, and made it very clear to him that, unless he gets help with his problem and resolves it, they will never get back together. She has also gone for counseling herself to see what she might be contributing to their situation. Acting this way can be very difficult, but it is acting responsibly.

The woman who allows her husband to physically abuse her or the children and doesn't do anything about it but complain is not acting responsibly. Staying in and putting up with this type of treatment is irresponsible. And the woman who year after year puts up with her husband's alcoholism and allows him to get away with it without serious consequences isn't acting responsibly, either.

It takes courage to act in these situations.

Doing nothing but blaming others for the difficulties we have may seem logical to hurting people. It may serve to justify one's own behavior, but it never resolves conflicts or problems. It only aggravates them.

Excuseitis—the failure to accept personal responsibility for what we have contributed to our difficulties—is one of the malignancies of today's society. We project blame onto others for what goes wrong as well as for what doesn't go right. We blame the past, the weather, our parents, mates, friends, the boss, the "other" woman, God, bad luck, lack of opportunity, the government, and a host of other things.

If I could impart to you only one truth that has the power to transform your life, it would be this: You are responsible!

Even if, perchance, we weren't responsible in any way for what went wrong in the past, what happened isn't nearly as important as how we reacted to what happened. For that we are totally responsible.

Teaching and accepting this principle is one of the greatest needs in today's society. If everybody acted responsibly, think how it would transform our world. If accepting personal responsibility is so vital, how can you ensure that you are acting responsibly?

❑ *First, accept the fact that you are responsible.*

Unless you believe you are responsible, you will never act responsibly. You will continue to want others to meet your needs and blame them for your problems. Accepting and believing that you are totally responsible for every area of your life is essential if you are going to overcome your losses, move forward to develop and reach your potential and make for yourself a bright and fulfilling future.

Regardless of what happened to us in the past (unless of course we have brain damage or are seriously handicapped), we are as adults fully responsible:

> for what we do about resolving our past
> for what we become
> for resolving our problems
> for getting our needs met in legitimate ways
> for our health
> for our happiness
> for our peace of mind
> for our emotions
> for our behavior
> for everything we do and feel

❏ *Second, choose responsibility.*

To be or not to be responsible is a choice each one of us makes. If we fail to choose to act responsibly, we have already chosen by default to act irresponsibly.

Two children can grow up in a dysfunctional home. Both can be deprived of love. One can remain bitter and resentful and allow his background to destroy his life. The other can accept what happened, face and resolve the damage it did, and make something great out of life. The difference is in one's attitude. It begins with the choice to accept personal responsibility.

❏ *Third, program responsibility thinking into your unconscious mind.*

To live and act responsibly without having to think about it, we need to program responsibility thinking into the right brain, the unconscious mind.

One of the most effective ways to do this is through repetition. Repeat to yourself the following affirmation: "I *am* responsible. I *am* responsible. I *am* responsible." Write this affirmation on a card. Tape it to your bathroom mirror, carry it in your pocket, and read and say it many times a day. The more you say it with feeling, the more it will be programmed into your unconscious mind and become a part of your personal value and belief system.

Once responsibility thinking has become a part of your belief system you will act on it automatically because, as we pointed out in an earlier chapter, people always act consistently with their beliefs. And the easiest, quickest, and most effective way to make responsibility thinking a part of your belief system is through repetition. "I *am* responsible." Say it over and over. Every day. For the rest of your life.

I have made responsibility thinking one of my personal goals and, along with my other goals and life purposes, write it out every day. This is another effective way to program it into the unconscious mind.

❏ *Finally, act responsibly.*

If you want to act responsibly and there is any doubt about whether you are doing so, ask yourself the question when making choices: "What is the responsible thing to do?" Think it through and act accordingly. When responsibility thinking is an integral part of your belief and value system and is programmed into your unconscious mind, it will be reinforced by consistently acting responsibly.

The acceptance of personal responsibility is absolutely essential for the healing of persons and our entire society. It is one of the highest marks of maturity.

19

Ask for Help When Needed

THE NORTH AMERICAN INDIANS had no written language before they met the white man. Their language, however, was far from primitive. Many of the Indians had as many words in their vocabulary as their English and French exploiters. Some of their words were much more picturesque, too. For example, "friend" to the Indians was "one-who-carries-my-sorrows-on-his-back."

Everybody needs at least one trusted Indian-type friend with whom he or she can share his or her deepest sorrows and painful feelings. We all need a helping hand and a listening ear when we're going through a difficult time. Here's how to get the help you need.

❑ *First, ask and you will receive.*

When you're hurting, don't be afraid to ask for help or for someone to listen to you. Choose an understanding friend with whom you feel safe to share your deepest pain and who will listen with genuine empathy and accept your feelings.

Every heartache, loss, and setback has within it the seeds of opportunity.

Very often (and this is especially true of men) we feel it is a sign of weakness to share our feelings, so we have a strong tendency to bottle them up and pay for it through ulcers, high blood pressure and other "dis-eases."

To share our sorrow is not a sign of weakness, but an indication of true strength, one of our greatest strengths being the ability and willingness to admit our weaknesses and show our humanness. It's more a sign of weakness *not* to admit our need of help when we need it and *not* to show our feelings when we're hurting.

Even married couples need a trusting friend other than their husband or wife with whom they can share their troubled feelings. No one person can ever meet all our needs. To think they can is very much a false expectation.

When sharing our feelings, we're not talking about "dumping" onto somebody else or confessing somebody else's "sins or faults," but a genuine opening up and expression of our own deepest feelings and heartaches to someone who cares, who listens, and who loves us still.

The kind of friend we all need is the kind that fits the old Arabian description of friendship: "A friend is one to whom we may pour out the contents of our hearts, chaff and grain together, knowing that the gentlest of hands will sift it, keep what is worth keeping and, with a breath of kindness, blow the rest away!"

❑ *Second, be selective.*

When choosing a friend with whom you can share your feelings, select one who won't tell you you shouldn't feel the way you do, judge you, have all the answers, have a need to "fix" you, or have a compulsion to give you advice.

The truth is that nobody has all the answers, neither can anybody "fix" anybody else but themselves, and there's just one problem with giving advice: it doesn't work. If it did, there wouldn't be any problems left in the world. Besides, if ten people offer you advice and direction, three will tell you to go north, three to go south, three east, and at least one west.

The kind of help you need is not advice. If you need direction, have friends help you see your options and encourage you to make your own decisions, as nobody else knows what you need to do more than you do yourself.

The answers you are seeking are ultimately to be found between you and God alone. They are not in luck, your environment, your upbringing (or lack of it) or in anything or anybody else.

The purpose of having a friend is to have someone you can talk to and who will give you loving support; someone who will be there for you; someone who will help you see your options; someone on whose shoulder you can cry; someone who will hug you when that's the thing that you need the most.

❑ *Third, find an encourager.*

Choose a friend or friends who are encouraging—who put courage into you. Avoid friends who are negative. They are not your friends at all. They are enemies because, instead of building you up, they pull you down and take courage out of you. Choose friends who are positive, who believe in you, who will be true supporters; those who know that you are going to come out a much wiser, gentler, more loving, and more whole person; friends who will assure you that you will survive and come through with flying colors. If you don't have such a friend to turn to, talk to your minister, family doctor, or a professional counselor.

❏ *Fourth, seek professional help.*

If your pain is too great and you feel overwhelmed, out of control, or that you are "coming unglued," don't hesitate to seek professional help. Your minister or doctor can advise you whom to see, or check the Yellow Pages under Counseling—Marriage, Family and Personal; Divorce Counseling; Organizations—Family Welfare; Psychotherapists; Psychologists; or Psychiatrists.

If you find yourself turning to alcohol or drugs to deaden your pain and especially if you are dwelling on thoughts of suicide, seek professional help immediately. If you don't know who to call, look up "Community: Personal and other emergencies" in the Yellow Pages.

Another reason to seek professional help is if you repeatedly find yourself in broken relationships. If this is so, there is every possibility that there is some unmet need or unresolved problem in yourself that is drawing you into these situations. Seek the help you need so you can break the chain.

Whatever you do, don't bear your burden alone. There's no need to. Ask for the help you need.

No matter how bad you feel or how much you are hurting, know that every heartache, loss, and setback has within it the seeds of some opportunity. Some of the greatest success stories are written by people who against seemingly overwhelming odds have accepted their trials and turned them into opportunities for personal growth and stepping stones on their pathway to success.

You can do the same. Choose friends who will empower you to do likewise.

20

Call on God
for Help

NOT SO LONG AGO when I was going through a time of loss myself, a friend sent me the following letter:

Dear Dick:
This time last year I went through a heart-wrenching experience due to the breakup of my family. What seemed like an eternal black cloud engulfing me is now behind me. I have [God] to be thankful for it.

I know he will carry your burdens for you also and be with you when you ask him to. I know the painful feelings you are facing now, but I am certain you will, in time, emerge a stronger, happier person.

Letters like this remind us how supportive friends as well as a religious faith can be at a time of deep sorrow.

For some reason or other most of us, even if we rarely ever darken the door of a church, call on God for help when we feel we're going under. That probably isn't the best way to practice one's faith, but it's better now than never. This is because faith in God can give you a power greater than your own to help you not only weather the storms of life, but to come through them a much better and stronger person.

Faith in God isn't meant to be an escape from pain. God doesn't overprotect those who believe in him. Neither does he function as a giant tranquilizer to be taken four times a day so you won't feel the pain. God doesn't work that way. The following are some of the ways that he does work in our lives and some of the benefits he provides to those who trust their life to him.

❏ *First, safety.*

While God doesn't protect us from the storms of life, he does bring us safely through them. That is, if we genuinely want him to, he will give us the wisdom and insight to help us better understand our sorrows, and the inner strength and courage to help us overcome them.

❏ *Second, confidence.*

God gives us a deep sense of confidence in his promise that no matter what happens to us—including receiving a broken heart—we know that he will use this and everything else that happens to us for a purpose.

This can, in the mouth of the insensitive person, sound trite. But, as the reflective comment of deep maturity and spiritual insight, it can also be true. As the apostle Paul said: "We know that all that happens to us is working for our good if we love God and are fitting into his plans."

❏ *Third, security.*

Knowing that God is vitally interested in every detail of our lives gives us a great sense of security. Jesus reminded us of this when he said:

Not one sparrow (What do they cost? Two for a cent?) can fall to the ground without your Father [God] knowing it. And the very hairs of your head are all numbered. So don't worry! You are more valuable to him than many sparrows.

❏ *Fourth, direction.*

God is almost always "telling" us something in every trial we face. Sometimes the only time he can get our attention is when we're hurting sufficiently to stop and listen.

When you are hurting, you can be sure that God has something to say to you, too—something that is for your good.

That has certainly been true in my life. On one occasion, God used an accident and a time in the hospital to "speak" to me and subsequently change the total direction of my life. Another time God used a major crisis and loss to expand my work and help me mature. He used still another loss to motivate me to write.

When you are hurting, you can be sure that God has something to say to you, too—something that is for your good. Ask God to help you hear what it is and to give you the courage to do what he is telling you to do. Whatever it is, you can be certain it will enrich your life.

❏ *Fifth, growth and maturity.*

As much as anything else, God wants to use your pain to help you understand yourself more fully and become a more mature person. This is so you will learn to love yourself, others, and God more fully and discover more meaningful and loving relationships.

You can make all the money in the world, become famous or achieve great success in any of a number of fields but, if you don't have someone to love and be loved by, what is the point of it all? People are not made to live in isolation. True, we don't have to be married to be happy, but we do need to have friends to love and love us. In fact, without love we will self-destruct.

Loving and intimate relationships, however, don't just happen. They are the result of growth and maturity which only come as we are open and honest and face ourselves as we really are. For many, if not most of us, the only thing that will motivate us to do this is pain. We cling tenaciously to our self-protective defenses which we hide behind and only let go of if we are hurting sufficiently.

As Tim Timmons and Charlie Hedges in their excellent book, *Call It Love or Call It Quits,* say about the need to jump the hurdles to effective communication (openness), purpose, and maturity:

> Some people have to come to the end of themselves, to hit bottom. For others, it takes a tragedy to motivate them: personal injury, financial crisis, a relational rejection or breakup, an accident, a hospital experience, a life-threatening disease, the loss of a loved one. Tragedy will often serve as a wake-up call.[11]

Let me assure you that God wants to use your loss as a wake-up call—a call to openness, growth, maturity, and love. James said in his letter:

Dear brothers, is your life full of difficulties and temptations? Then be happy, for when the way is rough, your patience has a chance to grow. So let it grow, and don't squirm out of your problems. For when your patience is finally in full bloom, then you will be ready for anything, strong in character, full and complete [mature].

Maturity, of course, takes time but, if we fail to take the opportunity our present pain gives us to face ourselves as we really are and move ahead to a greater level of maturity, we take the risk of having to face more heartache in the future. This is because we will bring it on ourselves and God will keep bringing us back to this point of self-confrontation in order that we might turn to him, face who we really are and grow. Or we take the risk of spending the rest of our lives hiding from ourselves and blindly living out our programming from the past. And then, tragically, instead of learning to live fully, we begin to die slowly.

As Albert Schweitzer once said: "The tragedy in life is not that we die, but rather what dies inside a man while he lives."

C. S. Lewis has said that our pain is God's megaphone by which he speaks to a deaf world. Without it, we would never bother to call him in the first place. How do we effectively respond to him?

The first step is to make a commitment of your life to Jesus Christ and respond to his open invitation to receive him into your life. This process enables us to become spiritually alive.

The second step is to allow God to use your pain to motivate you to grow towards maturity and discover the fullness of his love—for yourself, for others and for God. This is not to say our pain is good in itself. It isn't, but that experience, however difficult, can be used creatively by God, moving us into richer, more dynamic relationships.

❏ *Sixth, comfort.*

God wants you to know that he loves you in a very special way, that he genuinely wants you to come to him for help, and that he cares deeply about your sorrow.

Listen to his promise found in the Bible: "For God so loved the world that he gave his one and only Son, that whoever believes in him shall not perish but have eternal life."

Or again: "The steadfast love of the Lord never ceases, his mercies never come to an end; they are new every morning; great is your faithfulness."

The following passage from the book of Hebrews indicates the extent to which God empathizes with us, reaching out to us wherever we have been, whatever we have done:

> But Jesus the Son of God is our great High Priest who has gone to heaven itself to help us; therefore let us never stop trusting him. This High Priest of ours understands our weaknesses, since he had the same temptations we do, though he never once gave way to them and sinned. So let us come boldly to the very throne of God and stay there to receive his mercy and to find grace to help us in our times of need.

❏ *Seventh, care and understanding.*

God cares deeply about your sorrow. David said to God: "You have seen me tossing and turning through the night. You have collected all my tears and preserved them in your bottle! You have recorded every one in your book."

The prophet Isaiah wrote these comforting words about Jesus Christ, the Son of God:

> He was a man of sorrows and acquainted with grief.
> On the cross he bore the grief that was ours;
> there he carried our sorrows,
> there he was wounded for our transgressions,

there he was bruised for our sins.
The price of our peace was upon his shoulders
and by his wounds we are healed.

No one understands our sorrows and trials like Jesus. Nobody cares as much for us as he does. He is indeed a friend beyond comparison. He is the master healer of persons. Jesus himself said: "The Spirit of the Lord is upon me; he has appointed me to preach good news to the poor; he has sent me to heal the brokenhearted and to announce that . . . God is ready to give blessings to all who come to him."

Jesus also said, "Come to me, all you who are weary and burdened and I will give you rest. Take my yoke upon you and learn from me, for I am gentle and humble in heart, and you will find rest for your souls. For my yoke is easy and my burden is light."

Remember that God loves you with an everlasting love. He wants you to come to him for help, he wants you to know that he cares deeply about your sorrow, and he wants to heal your wounded heart and life. As somebody else put it: "God will mend even a broken heart if you will give him all the pieces."

If you give your life to God and genuinely want him to make you whole, he will not only mend your broken heart, but will help you grow and, in his good time, make something beautiful out of your life.

Endnotes

1. Henri J. M. Nouwen, *The Wounded Healer,* Image Books, 1972, p. 66.

2. Robert Fulghum, *All I Really Need to Know I Learned in Kindergarten,* quoted from *Encounter* Magazine, ACTS International, November 1987, p. 5.

3. Bernie S. Siegel, *Love, Medicine & Miracles,* Harper & Row, 1986, pp. 27–28.

4. Frank Minirth, Paul Meier, Don Hawkins, *Worry-Free Living,* Thomas Nelson, 1989, pp. 22–23.

5. Emmett Miller, "In Helping Others to Succeed," *Insight,* Issue 88, Nightingale Conant, 1990, p. 42.

6. Terry Hershey, *Beginning Again,* Thomas Nelson, 1986, p. 163.

7. Nouwen, *The Wounded Healer,* p. 87.

8. David Stoop, *Self Talk: Key to Personal Growth,* Fleming H. Revell Company, 1982, back cover.

9. Adapted from Iona Henry McLaughlin, *Triumph Over Tragedy,* Abingdon, 1957.

10. Melba Colgrove, Harold H. Bloomfield, and Peter McWilliams, *How to Survive the Loss of a Love,* Bantam, 1976, p. 68.

11. Tim Timmons and Charlie Hedges, *Call It Love or Call It Quits,* Worthy Publishing, 1988, p. 21.